Boomtowns of Shasta Dam

A History of Central Valley, Project City, Summit City, Toyon and Shasta Dam Village, 1937-1993

by
Al M. Rocca
Faculty Advisor, CalStateTeach
California State University, Monterey Bay

Renown Publishing

Redding, California

www.renownpublishing.com

Author: Rocca, Al M.
Boomtowns of Shasta Dam:
A History of Central Valley, Project City, Summit City,
Toyon and Shasta Dam Village, 1937-1993
Non-Fiction, 147 pages
1. Communities—West (U.S.)—History.
2. 1930s & 1940s—West (U.S.)—History. I Title.

First Printing: 1993
(Redding Museum of Art & History)
Second Edition: 2012

ISBN: 0-9643378-9-4   (10 digit)   ISBN: 978-0-9643378-9-3 (13 digit)

Library of Congress Cataloging Number: 2011918231

All photos are used with permission from the United States Bureau of Reclamation, Shasta Historical Society, and the author, unless otherwise noted. In particular, the author wishes to extend its gratitude to the Jeremy Tuggle and Jay Thompson at the Shasta Historical Society, and Sheri Harral and Tami Corn at the U.S. Bureau of Reclamation, and to private individuals who offered their photographs. Cover Photograph Credit: Shasta Historical Society. Quoted material is referenced in-text and credited at the end of the book.

Al M. Rocca is Professor Emeritus, Simpson University in Redding, California. He has published numerous local history books on northern California including: *Shasta Dam: A History of Construction, 1938-1945*, *America's Master Dam Builder: The Engineering Genius of Frank T. Crowe* and *Whiskeytown National Recreation Area: A History*. These books are available at: www.amazon.com

Table of Contents

BOOMTOWN
CENTER
"The Hub of Commercial Activity"
Water Service Now Available
Choice Business Locations And
Ideal Homesites

Preface

President Franklin Delano Roosevelt visited Redding, California, on September 23, 1932. Al M. Rocca, historian and local author, takes the occasion of the President's visit to be the starting point of his book *Boomtowns of Shasta Dam*. The construction of Shasta Dam during the Great Depression is the backdrop for the book, a topic Rocca has documented in a previous book. The focus of this study is the people who built the dam and the communities they formed. It is the story of the founding and early growth of Boomtown (a.k.a., Central Valley, Shasta Lake City); Midway (Project City); Summit City, Toyon; and other communities that came into being when workers from across the nation poured into the north state to participate in the monumental task of building the center piece of the Central Valley Project.

As a great-great grandson of William Joshua Hammans who, along with his son Earl Eugene Hammans, founded Project City (initially not much more than a pit stop for truckers known as Midway), I was delighted to learn details when reading Rocca's book about the role these ancestors of mine played in the growth and development of this community. The index to Rocca's book is chock-full of the names of people who were early inhabitants of these towns and either worked on the dam or played a role in the economy that came to life amidst the bustle of the construction effort. No doubt many others will share the thrill I experienced when reading this book, as Rocca adds color and context to the lives our forebears led.

The initial edition of this book quickly sold out. The new version comes with a new Introduction and includes photos that were not in the original. As a historian, I have found this book to be a valuable addition to our understanding of local history. People working on family histories will continue to find this book most helpful. Given the attention to detail and the accuracy of the reporting, the book will also be of interest to scholars studying New Deal policies and the historical impact of the measures implemented.

Jeremy M. Tuggle
Local historian and author
December 2011

Introduction
Tami Corn, Public Tour Supervisor
United States Bureau of Reclamation

Shasta Dam is an incredible place—15 million tons of concrete holding back over a trillion gallons of water—and it stands as the second largest concrete dam in the Unites States and among the largest man-made structures on earth. Shasta Dam provides flood control for the upper Sacramento River valley, which was prone to devastating seasonal floods, and water storage for a growing and thirsty state. It also produces clean, efficient, and inexpensive hydroelectricity.

Beyond the concrete and water and the wires and watts, Shasta Dam has another story to tell. This is the story of the hardworking, industrious men and women who came here to find a remote, but beautiful area at the foothills of the Siskiyou and Cascade Mountains. They came in droves from Oklahoma and Arkansas, looking for a chance at a new life. Many were refugees from the Dust Bowl, a devastating drought-induced calamity in the Midwest. They had watched their family farms and dreams dry up and blow away with the relentless winds. Eager to find a way to survive, these hardy folks traveled across the country to find a job, and hope. They found that hope and a new place to call home.

The area was mostly chaparral; covered in manzanita, pine, and oaks. Prior to the building of Shasta Dam, the area was mostly known because of the train depot—and its location along the major north-south route of the Southern Pacific rail line. Due to its rural location, Shasta County was particularly hard hit during the Great Depression, and even though Redding, California, was the major town in the county, it, too, suffered during this time. With the building of the massive dam just north of Redding, the county was going to change and with some forethought, grow in a big way.

Shasta Dam was built during Roosevelt's New Deal era—a time when many of the country's big dams were built as part of a National program to build infrastructure and put people to work, boosting the economy of a depressed country. Many of the workers who migrated to the area had spent time working on other big dams, such as Hoover and Grand Coulee. Shasta was going to be the last of these big dams, and many of these folks were looking to settle down and make roots in a new community.

To house the workers, the contractors of Pacific Constructors Incorporated built a "village" just downstream from the dam site to house the workers, men and women, who came to the area. The construction camp included 139 homes for married families, as well as large dormitories to house the single men. They had their own commissary, recreation room, and mess hall. A state-of-the-art hospital was built to address the health care needs of the residents. The model community of Toyon rose from the manzanita brush, just a few miles away from the dam site, to house the Bureau of Reclamation supervisors and engineers.

While the dam brought a new life for the many workers who were building it, many others got in on the new-found opportunity for prosperity. Industrious developers started buying up land and selling lots to many of the dam workers. From these little developments, built to address the need of housing in the area, came the communities of Summit City, Project City, and Central Valley (now the City of Shasta Lake). With this housing also came businesses to provide shopping and services for the growing population. People were moving in and settling on this new frontier.

The builders of Shasta Dam were a no-nonsense, honest, hardworking group of people, and they saw the opportunity to make a life here in their new home state of California. Neighbor helping neighbor, these communities continued to grow even after the dam was completed. As the saying goes, "They came to build a dam but stayed to build a community." This is so very true.

Today, it is not hard to find the families of those dam builders, if not the dam builders themselves, at the local grocery store, bank, or post office. They built and settled these towns, raised their families, and chose to call this place home. The history and pride of the community of Shasta Lake is all around you as you walk the streets—good people with a story to tell.

This book tells the tale of these towns that started out as boomtowns from a construction era and managed to live on, transitioning into a modern community but still maintaining and honoring its humble and simple beginning. Dr. Rocca has done exhaustive research on these towns and really captured the spirit of not only the communities but also the people that make them up. His thorough study has produced a very compelling story—one fitting the incredible undertaking of building Shasta Dam. This is not the story of concrete and water or wires and watts but of the people and the place, they call home.

Tami Corn

November, 2011

Shasta Dam Boomtowns

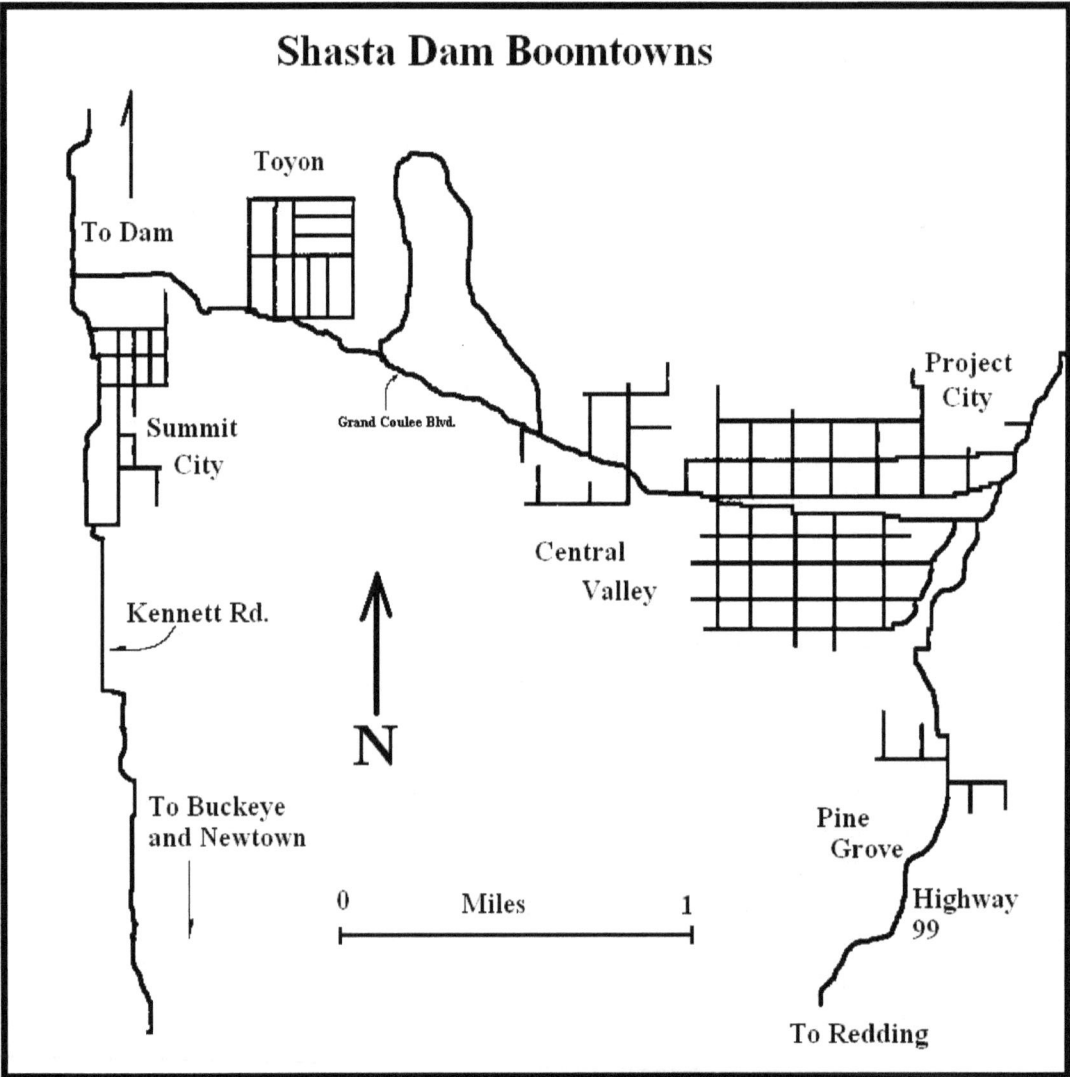

Toyon

To Dam

Grand Coulee Blvd.

Summit
City

Project
City

Central
Valley

Kennett Rd.

N

To Buckeye
and Newtown

Pine
Grove

Highway
99

0	Miles	1

To Redding

Chapter 1
The Central Valley Project

On September 23, 1932, 3,000 citizens of Redding, California, mostly Democrats, stood anxiously at the town train depot awaiting arrival of a special 11:00 a.m. express. It carried an honored guest. These curious northern Californians did not have long to wait. At 11:09, the train arrived, and within minutes, officials set up a loudspeaker system on the portico of the last railroad car. As the crowd pushed forward for a better listening position, a familiar figure emerged onto the portico. It was Judge Francis Carr, chairman of the 1932 Democratic Committee for Shasta County. He traveled north earlier in the day to meet the honored guest, Franklin Delano Roosevelt, to discuss economic problems in the state with him, and to prepare his introduction to the people of Shasta County.

The gathered crowd had been discussing the economic plight that had gripped much of northern California since the end of World War I. They had seen little of the Coolidge prosperity, as the copper smelters of the war years had by then, all shut down. Several eager citizens debated the pros and cons of the honored guest's "New Deal" proposals that he had been espousing on his cross-country trek. All of the candidate's earlier political statements in newspaper articles contained few details of his program; or, how it would benefit northern California.

The "Great Crash of '29" brought serious economic problems to Shasta County, an already depressed area. As the Depression wore on, local Red Cross representatives distributed food to the needy, while ten delegates from Redding took part in a hunger march on the state capitol. Despite the hardships of the current economic environment, some residents hoped that rumors concerning the building of a large dam would bring a brighter economic future. One man in 1931 declared that he was going to buy new clothes, a new car, books, and be finished with "being depressed."[1]

Judge Carr, worried about the declining economic climate of the region, introduced Franklin Delano Roosevelt, as the "next President of the United States."[2] Roosevelt, clutching the railing of the back portico for support, delivered his message in less than five minutes. While Roosevelt gave no specifics, he did indicate that northern California would share in New Deal legislation. He finished his comments by promising, "Friends, we shall have beer."[3]

By April of 1933 Redding did have beer, as did most of the nation, and local residents celebrated the repeal of the Eighteenth Amendment. That month a local newspaper reported:

> President Roosevelt today approved establishment of 628 camps (Civilian Conservation Corps) for the western states. This time Shasta County was included in the C.C.C. Shasta County leads with eleven camps.[4]

However, the C.C.C. camps did little to help relieve the depressed northern counties of California. Judge Carr decided to follow-up an idea that he had talked about with Roosevelt on that train ride the year before. That idea concerned the building of a large dam on the upper Sacramento River, something Californians had debated for at least two decades.

Judge Francis Carr (Shasta Historical Society)

Later that year, Judge Carr and John McColl, a successful dairyman and newly elected state senator, journeyed to Washington D.C. to lobby for a Redding area dam. The dam, they argued, would not only provide jobs, but also stop the frequent flooding in the area, generate electricity, provide for new irrigated acreage, and help regulate salinity levels in the delta region.

Senator John McColl (Shasta Historical Society)

While their immediate results were not apparent at the national level, their proposals joined with other water bills in the state legislature, and passed in 1933 as the Central Valley Project Act. Within three years, President Roosevelt approved plans for the great Central Valley Project, and Congress soon thereafter, provided funds to build massive Shasta Dam, which would be the "keystone" of the entire project. Carr and McColl, jubilant over the decision to build the dam, never realized that the dam project would also spawn three new permanent communities.

Judge Carr's lobbying, part of a united effort by many local and state agencies, signaled the climax of a concerted campaign to solve California's water problems—a campaign that had extensive historical roots. Concern for the lack of water and the need to consider building irrigation works in California's Central Valley, date back to the 1850s. The gold rush era spawned numerous small local irrigation works, usually canals, by private interest groups. These attempts focused on redistributing available water from the Sacramento and San Joaquin Rivers to tracts of promising land lying to the east and west. Most of these early endeavors developed independent of each other, resulting in a plethora of water-rights court cases at the local and the state level. It became clear that the final

11

solution focus on the immediate implementation of an overall state water plan.

The Army Corps of Engineers prepared a comprehensive water plan for the state in 1873.[5] From then until the early twentieth century, the Army Engineers, and at times, the Reclamation Service, revised and enlarged numerous irrigation plans. However, once again, water-rights litigation stifled effective action.

In 1919, Colonel Robert Bradford Marshall, a geographer for the United States Geological Survey and the Reclamation Service, published a pamphlet entitled *Irrigation of Twelve Million Acres in the Valley of California*. Marshall called for a complete consolidation of the state's local irrigation projects. The statewide project engineers planned the construction of a huge dam, at a strategic location somewhere near the headwaters of the Sacramento River. The resulting flow would then run naturally to the lowlands around the capital, then uphill (using pumps) to southern California.[6]

Marshall failed in his attempt to have the state legislature authorize the money for his plans. However, the pamphlet did initiate a period of further state water studies. In 1921, the legislature made the first of a series of appropriations for investigate plans for the conservation, control, storage, distribution, and application of all waters of the state. By 1931, the Division of Water Resources submitted to the legislature a comprehensive plan for utilizing the water resources of the Central Valley.

This proposal, the Central Valley Project, received ratification from the California legislature in 1933 and appeared on a referendum for voter approval that December.[7] Revenue bonds, sold against the expected power and irrigation water sales, were supposed to provide financing for the project. The state sold few bonds, however, since the Great Depression discouraged investments. State Engineer Edward Hyatt then tried to interest the federal government into backing the project.[8] After extended meetings, he agreed with Public Works Administration officials that the Bureau of Reclamation should take overall command of the project, bidding out work on the components of the project (i.e., dams, canals, irrigation works) to private contractors. Robert Kelley's *Battling the Inland Sea* argued that the New Dealers had become convinced that many of the water irrigation projects promoted by the earlier Progressives were worthwhile endeavors, and urged the injection of huge sums of money to build "very large headwater dams."[9] Kelley noted that the decision to construct huge multi-purpose concrete dams signaled a major policy transition within the federal government, previously funding only small irrigation dams.[10]

The Central Valley Project, authorized in the Rivers and Harbors Act (August 30, 1935), had as its centerpiece damming the Sacramento River, in the north end of the Central Valley and the San Joaquin River, in the southern portion of the great valley. Plans called for water, from Shasta Dam (originally called Kennett) near Redding, to flow down canals to areas in need of a stable water source. The law intended the Tehama-Colusa Canal to supply water for the extreme western portion of the Sacramento Valley, an area potentially very productive, and the Friant-Kern Canal was supposed to bring the precious liquid south through Tulare and Kern Counties to Bakersfield. Numerous other smaller dams, canals, pumping stations, conduits, and electrical transmission lines would supplement the main construction and unify the entire valley.

John C. Page, Commissioner, Bureau of Reclamation (Bureau of Reclamation)

The Bureau of Reclamation began preliminary fieldwork on the project in November 1935. Actual site construction of camp facilities, support buildings, road grading, and other work moved into full gear by October of 1937. Excavation at the Shasta Dam site and work on relocating the Southern Pacific railroad lines around the proposed Shasta reservoir in late 1939 helped to employ several hundred hopeful job seekers.[11]

The abandoned town of Kennett remained a vibrant copper mining town until the 1920s. (Bureau of Reclamation)

Shasta Dam, architecturally engineered by the Bureau of Reclamation as a massive concrete structure, became the keystone of the entire Central Valley Project; second only to Hoover Dam in height and to Grand Coulee in width. Such an enormous undertaking attracted national attention, with numerous construction companies seeking to land lucrative government contracts. The enormous size of the dam project precluded most, if not all, private construction companies from tackling the venture singly. In addition, government acceptance of the bids remained contingent on the builder securing bonds totaling millions of dollars. Surety companies, underwriters for the costly bonds, themselves required that, "cash sufficient to finance the contract be raised and impounded under joint

14

control of surety and contractor."[12] In addition, bidding companies needed to provide proof of financial stability and successful prior job experience.

Obviously, very few construction companies could satisfy government stipulations. The result of this—the joint venture—had by 1938 become common practice.[13] The federal government encouraged joint venture bids, since they resulted in a greater spectrum of bidding organizations, usually producing lower bids.

The Six Companies, which had successfully bid on Hoover Dam, completed the project on schedule, and secured a handsome profit for shareholders. In December 1937, while Henry Kaiser's Six Companies prepared its bid on Grand Coulee Dam, a newly formed corporation, Pacific Constructors, Inc., put its own bid together.

One of the original owners of Pacific Constructors, J.C. Maguire, recalled the genesis of this new firm. William A. Johnson of Los Angeles, one of the industry leaders in Southern California with large holdings in a number of construction enterprises, took the lead in getting the business leaders together. After informal discussions with several prominent Los Angeles contractors, he called a meeting which Steve Griffith, President of Griffith Company, L.E. Dixon, head of the company bearing his name, Clyde Wood, President of the newly formed Metropolitan Construction Company and Floyd Shofner of Shofner, Gordon & Hinman attended. The joint bid proposal on Grand Coulee Dam received an enthusiastic response from everyone in attendance and construction executives moved forward with plans for a bidding strategy. As progress continued, others builders received invitations to join the venture including D.W. Thruston, a newcomer to Los Angeles with years of successful operation and experience on heavy construction in the Middle West, Lawler & Maguire of Butte, Montana, Joseph V. Hogan (Arundel Corporation), and Hunkin-Conkey Construction, an old and well-known firm of Cleveland, Ohio. All the above-mentioned companies accepted the invitation to join the new organization. This gathering of companies formed the original Pacific Constructors group.[14]

By bidding too high on their first try, Pacific Constructors lost the Grand Coulee contract to the veteran group Six Companies. The difference between the bids totaled eight million dollars—a significant amount—yet it set up conditions that ultimately allowed Pacific Constructors to win the bid for Shasta Dam. Maguire noted that Six Companies, believing that Pacific Constructors would again bid high, was lulled into "a false sense of security,"[15] and they bid higher than usual on the Shasta job. The bids revealed a difference of $262,907 on a thirty-six million dollar project, in favor of Pacific Constructors.[16]

Immediately upon winning the Shasta bid, Pacific Constructors reorganized, adding new members, an Executive Committee and electing a

General Superintendent of Construction.[17] Frank Crowe, with over thirty years of dam building experience, including Hoover and Parker Dams, won the job. Crowe not only brought his invaluable experience with him to the Shasta project, but he also brought his "well—oiled" construction crew— organized and eager to take on the challenge of a new dam in northern California. Many of Crowe's men and Pacific Constructors' personnel would make new homes in the Shasta boomtowns. Some continued to live in the area after completion of the dam and still do today. Others moved on to new construction projects in the West.

Frank Crowe, Superintendent of Construction of Shasta Dam (Bureau of Reclamation)

The Bureau of Reclamation encountered little difficulty in obtaining the land for the dam site. Consisting of steep-sloped canyons, digger pine, manzanita, and scrub oak, the location had little other use. Its climate is a unique mixture of unusually high rainfall in the winter, up to 108 inches, and hot temperatures in the summer, with daytime highs well over 100 degrees Fahrenheit. To the north, beautiful snow-capped Mt. Shasta provides the illusion that the dam site is located in mountain country, when actually its elevation is only 550 feet above sea level.

Historically, the Sacramento River served as a transportation corridor between the rugged mountainous Pacific Northwest and California's interior valley. Michael La Franboise, a Hudson Bay Company employee, opened the "Sacramento Trail" in 1831 and French and Canadian fur trappers traversed it regularly. Indians eventually shut down the trail until 1855 when Ross McCloud reopened an improved trail on the west side of the river.[18]

California gold miners poured through this area in the early 1850s as the tributaries of the Sacramento River became a favorite destination for hopeful miners. With the building of the railroad through this region (1883-1886), communities of varying sizes took root, almost all based on mineral extraction. The largest of these mountain mining communities were Keswick, Coram, and Kennett (near dam site). Beginning in 1896 the copper smelters in the area attracted hundreds of unemployed persons, including large numbers of Italian workers. After World War I, the demand for defense related copper products declined, and the smelters along with the towns folded up. The last of them, Kennett, was abandoned by 1919.[19]

The Bureau of Reclamation did make good use of the old Buckeye-Kennett Road that provided a necessary link to Redding. This road, plus a new one cut in from Highway 99, assured easy access for Bureau inspectors and contracting engineers as they considered preliminary plans for rerouting the Southern Pacific Railroad by building a Sacramento diversion tunnel and laying out the government and contractor's camps in late 1937. By then word had gone out and hundreds of Depression-weary workers and their families had migrated to the dam site—Redding area—and were anxiously awaiting employment notices.

Dignitaries on hand for the ground-breaking ceremonies (September 1937) on the Shasta Dam project included (left to right): Earl Kelly, Director, California State Dept. of Public Works; Helene May Bacon Boggs, Shasta County pioneer, John C. Page, Commissioner, Bureau of Reclamation (Bureau of Reclamation).

Official party of the Department of the Interior—subcommittee (and family members) of the United States House of Representatives (Appropriations Committee). The committee members attended the same ceremonies noted above in September of 1937 (Bureau of Reclamation).

18

Chapter 2
New Arrivals and Early Settlements

As early as 1934 construction stiffs on Boulder Dam (later renamed Hoover Dam) heard about the Central Valley Project. The news created much excitement, as word spread of the beautiful natural surroundings where Kennett Dam (later renamed Shasta) would be located. To the workers living in the high desert of Boulder City the thought of working and living in a fresh pine-scented mountain environment provided great incentive to migrate early, in the hopes of securing a home site and a job.

The exact number of migrants moving into Shasta County is not certain. By January of 1938, 1860 persons had registered at the Redding branch office of the United States Employment Service.[1] Most job seekers who arrived in the vicinity of the dam site put up temporary homesteads and waited for hiring to begin. At first, they drove in on Highway 99 and set up tents along both sides of the Sacramento River north of Redding. Much local resentment arose as hungry "Okies" and "Arkies" roamed the streets of Redding during the day in hopes of acquiring part-time jobs or, at least, some food and clothing.[2]

On December 7, 1937, the Redding City Council urged the federal government to begin work as soon as possible, since hundreds of skilled and unskilled men waited anxiously for hiring to start. The council complained that relief rolls swelled to dangerously high levels creating a "most serious situation."[3] That same day, R.M. Snell, district supervisor for the Bureau of Reclamation, gave a sobering talk at a Kiwanis luncheon. He stated that hundreds of job hopefuls would have to wait six months before preliminary excavation at the dam site would be completed, and large-scale hiring for concrete work would occur.[4]

By September of 1938, the trickle of migrants turned into a flood as thousands of laid-off dam workers from Grand Coulee, Ft. Peck, Parker, and Hoover Dam sought new jobs. These newcomers spread out along the many tributaries of the Sacramento and near recently graded roads heading toward the dam site. United States Bureau of Reclamation personnel estimated that several hundred "home" camps, some containing five or more families, were within a ten-mile radius of the proposed dam site.[5]

These temporary camps took many forms. Initially, trailers and tents of every possible size and shape blossomed into view around the dam site. A simple clearing in the manzanita brush located most temporary homes. The settlers erected tents, constructed rough homes from scrap lumber, or lived in trailers.

Temporary tent camps appeared all over the area north of Redding to the construction site (Shasta Historical Society).

At least one visitor to the Shasta Dam area during 1938-39 reeled from what he termed "the shock of the abject poverty and hopelessness prevalent in the camps." Writing for an Oxnard newspaper, the article later appeared in a Redding newspaper and received much criticism from the editor for an "unbridled imagination run riot with no attempt at fact."[6] The article painted a bleak picture of squatter life. There was "no sanitation, water had to be hauled for miles, women with babies gaunt eyed and half-starved hoping and praying their husbands may get on at the dam."[7] The article described the hundreds of job seekers arriving daily, taxing ability of Redding to support such a rapid influx of population. Rumors of rampant crime in and around the camps spread. However, surviving residents do not recall that crime was a prevalent camp problem. In fact, many noted a congenial and safe environment, as neighbor helped neighbor sharing food and supplies. The article continued with references to the outbreak of diphtheria and typhoid spreading rapidly through the camps. Relief finally came from locally donated serum.

The rough living conditions apparent in the camps paralleled the situation that occurred ninety years before when thousands of gold seekers hit Shasta County creeks to strike it rich. Like their mid-twentieth century counterparts, these nineteenth century gold seekers crowded along the same creeks. These boomtowners of the Old Shasta mining camp, located just a few miles away from the new dam developments, had in their day, slept in tents too. They experienced the same kind of hunger and extreme anxiety. They saw numerous diseases sweep through their town, devastating all age groups, but particularly the young. They lived in the mud and snow in the winter, and suffered through the long hot summers of Shasta County. They also built a boomtown (Shasta) that survived the gold rush boom years to become a successful contemporary community.[8]

Solid data are not available, but apparently many, if not most, early arrivals and subsequent dam workers arrived in the area as complete families. However, hundreds of eager job seekers were single men, living together in the camps in numbers ranging from two, to more than twenty. Bachelors possessed five of the basic necessities held in common by all Depression migrants: car, tent, folding table, wash basin, and cooking utensils. Often bachelors went in together and shared the price for gasoline and automobile upkeep. Married men with families abounded also, a fact suggested by over 100 interviews with dam workers. It appears that married men who had previously worked on dams, and therefore possessed necessary skills for specific jobs, felt confident of another opportunity. These men also retained personnel connections with Frank Crowe, Superintendent for Pacific Constructors, a stern hard-driving task master who rewarded hard-working men with another job.

One of the most difficult problems for early arrivals to overcome was that of securing an adequate water supply. Many families set up residence on or near the Sacramento River. When this was no longer possible, due to the cramped conditions by early 1938, migrants accumulated on both sides of the main road leading from State Highway 99 west to the proposed dam site. Later this main avenue, Grand Coulee Boulevard, served as the nucleus for the development of the commercial boomtowns. Initial well drilling revealed, a large hard-rock strata covering much of the impacted area. Struggling early settlers carried their water supply in from nearby sources.

With government construction of preliminary buildings including workshops, storage facilities, dormitories, and Government Camp (Toyon) in late 1938, hundreds of newly hired workers utilized scrap lumber in an effort to construct more permanent type shelters before winter set in. Using truckloads of scrap lumber, home builders constructed simple straight-forward shelters.

Many of these families had previously lived in temporary camps. Others were quite young and had no prior dam work qualifications. Life was particularly hard on women; yet, none complained about their physical situation. On the contrary, many considered themselves fortunate to be living in northern California; all stated that they had confidence that the Shasta job would provide work for years to come.

Living conditions proved rugged for families as they waited for hiring on Shasta Dam to begin (Shasta Historical Society).

Several hundred school age children roamed the campsites. They helped with chores around the camp or played with other children from nearby campsites. Most had little previous schooling. As soon as a school did become available near Government Camp (Toyon), parents made a concerted effort to send their children to school. They also contributed time developing a strong Parent Teachers Association (P.T.A.). In fact, the Toyon and Central Valley P.T.A. groups later provided a social foundation upon which the boomtowns would synthesize community spirit.[9]

The pattern of camp locations helped determine the eventual location of the Shasta Dam boomtowns. The initial camps, located on the north bank of the Sacramento River, near Redding, reflected the desire of families to be close to part-time job sources, food, and information concerning the building of Shasta Dam. Since the Bureau of Reclamation headquarters issued job postings from the Redding office, it made sense to remain near enough to check hiring opportunities regularly. Several Redding residents remembered throngs of "Okies" and "Arkies" drifting through town in search of any kind of jobs—usually jobs that traded work for food.[10]

"Drifters" came by the hundreds, then thousands to Shasta County in anticipation of employment on Shasta Dam. Many were single men or married men without their families (Bureau of Reclamation).

The number of "Dust Bowl" drifters living in and around Redding is difficult to pin down. Redding citizens estimated in late 1938 early 1939 the number of newcomers ranged between a couple hundred to several thousand. News of the project had spread rapidly via newspapers, radio, and anxious conversation, and now federal inspectors and Pacific Constructors personnel arrived by the dozens and added to the growing ranks of new county residents. All of this activity placed tremendous pressure on Redding housing. Most new arrivals, with little or no funds to purchase housing or pay for monthly apartment rentals, now drifted closer to the actual dam site, eagerly anticipating work. Camps spread along both sides of the Sacramento River northward to Kennett, stringing out to include the many small tributaries.

The two main transportation routes into the proposed site, Buckeye Road and the new government graded Shasta Dam Boulevard, received hundreds of job hopefuls, with prime locations secured jobs on a first-come first-serve basis.[11] As can be determined from the map on page 8, the boomtowns originated close to the dam site and along these two major roads. In addition, the Bureau of Reclamation had already begun to lay out government camp at Toyon, providing further incentive for unemployed migrants to house themselves near "the action." This new arrival settlement pattern is reminiscent of Boulder and Grand Coulee Dam sites. Migrants assumed that their job prospects increased in relation to their location to the job site. As it turned out, the Bureau and Pacific Constructors did locate hiring offices at the dam site.

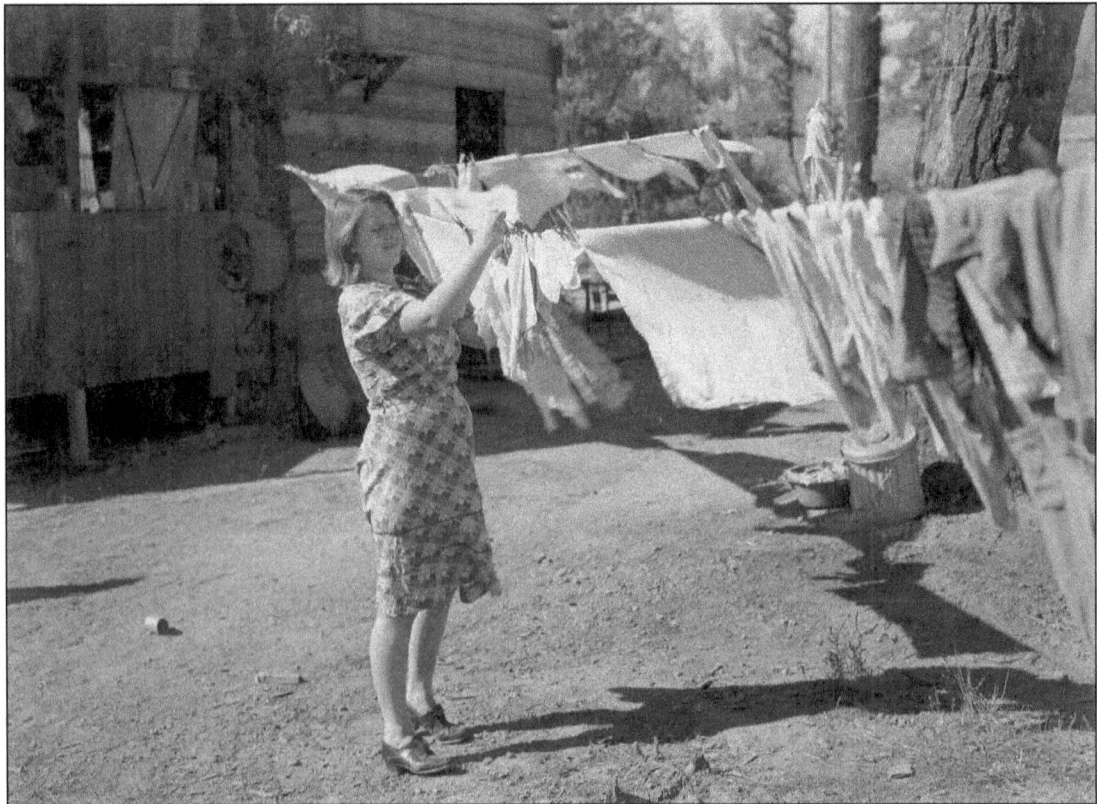

Daily life proved difficult as families dealt the temporary nature of their camps and lack of running water and electricity (Bureau of Reclamation).

Abandoned automobiles appear along roads leading into the construction area, as few families could afford to repair damaged cars and trucks (Bureau of Reclamation).

This photo shows Grand Coulee Blvd, heading west from Highway 99—leading to the dam site. On the left, work continues on the Dama Grande Inn (Bureau of Reclamation).

Chapter 3
U. S. Government Town (Toyon)

The Bureau of Reclamation by 1930 could look back over a long tradition of dam building in the West. The initial step in each project, whether a dam in Colorado, a levee in Texas, or a canal in Arizona, involved the construction of temporary residences for its workers. No standard policy appears to have existed to explain the extent of this federal responsibility. Sometimes elaborate and extensive quarters were constructed as in the case of Boulder Dam. Here the government became involved in community planning, hiring a city manager to oversee policy. Prior to this however, most government housing at Bureau jobs consisted of tents, tenthouses and modest wooden structures. Before Hoover Dam, most Bureau projects were relatively small and did not require years to finish. Everyone knew that they would be moving on to a new work location, usually within a few months. Hoover Dam, then, set a new precedent in government housing participation for Bureau projects. Now with huge multi-year endeavors being undertaken throughout the Depression years, government investment in project housing rose tremendously.

As construction moved ahead on the Shasta Dam Government Town (Toyon) in September and October of 1938, it soon became apparent that the Boulder City model of development would not be repeated in northern California. Whereas Boulder City fused the government inspector residences with privately owned homes and businesses, Toyon was strictly for housing government inspectors, managers, and engineers, as well as their families. No privately owned residences or businesses were allowed. The reason for this change is not clear, but, one government representative, Lyn Parker,[12] believed that while the government pointed to Boulder City as a great success story in the area of New Deal community planning, problems plagued the heavily subsidized construction town. Parker stated that at Shasta, the Bureau was primarily interested in moving ahead with the dam construction and not in experimenting with community development. In addition, the Bureau had appointed Ralph Lowry, an assistant inspector at Boulder Dam, to run the new Shasta Dam government camp and Lowry did not want the added burdens of administering another Boulder City.[13]

Ralph Lowry, Chief Bureau of Reclamation Engineer on Shasta Dam and Administrator of Toyon (Bureau of Reclamation).

Toyon was laid out two miles from the dam site and boasted a well-planned street pattern, standardized construction methods, and accompanying landscaping. The landscaping designed by Wilbur Weed included lawns, trees, and shrubs. The orderly appearance of Toyon, particularly during the first few years (1938-1945), offered a stark comparison to the haphazard growth and nonstandard building methods seen in the three boomtowns.

The United States Bureau of Reclamation headquarters building dominated the architecture of Toyon and commanded the immediate attention of pedestrians and motorists using the main thoroughfare, Shasta Dam Boulevard. Bureau headquarters opened in September of 1938. From here, the overall guidance for the construction of Shasta Dam took place. Ralph Lowry managed Toyon. Entrance to and the exit from Toyon was carefully planned to flank both sides of the Bureau headquarters, although Toyon residents witnessed little social or culture interference by the Bureau.[14]

Bureau of Reclamation Headquarters at Toyon (Bureau of Reclamation)

Housing at Toyon, like Boulder City, included single men's dormitories, duplexes, and single family residences set out in formalized rectangular blocks. Among the first two buildings to appear on the scene, the two-storied single men's dormitories loomed large over the construction

28

site. Curious onlookers noted that these giant dormitories announced the government's intention to change the local landscape in a big way. The simple and orderly landscaping around the dormitories and single family homes presented an attractive environment for workers and their families. Much of the landscaping had been worked and installed by Civilian Conservation Corps (C.C.C.) enrollees.[15]

Bureau boarders in the single men's dormitories did not pay rent,[16] but meals had to be obtained elsewhere. In fact, with the contractor's mess hail over two miles away, most government employees regularly patronized small newly built "hash houses' and diners in nearby burgeoning Summit City.[17] A group of single men, later with Lowry's permission, utilized one of the small single family residences to organize a bachelor's club with the primary intent of offering hot meals within the government compound.[18]

Single men's dormitories recently completed (Bureau of Reclamation)

The duplexes and single family residences ranged in size from small one-bedroom models for entry level government assistants to roomier two-bedroom homes for higher level federal inspectors, such as Ralph Lowry.

Rent for the one-bedroom homes hovered around thirty dollars a month and included all utilities.

While the commercial boomtowns' growth would be hampered by inadequate utilities, Toyon residents, from the start, realized full utility service, becoming the envy of residents in surrounding areas. The Bureau purchased power from Pacific Gas & Electric (P. G. & E.) and ran power lines to each home. A huge water storage tank on a nearby hill supplied year-round quality water to individual homes. A central sewer system operated from the beginning. The system maintained by bureau workers provided trouble free operation for many years. Bureau employees even disposed of garbage. Electric heating ensured warm indoor environments for government workers during the long cold winters of northern California. In contrast, most early boomtown settlers chopped oak or cedar wood for use in hand-constructed rock fireplaces or crude Franklin stoves.

Family home construction in Toyou, 1938 (Bureau of Reclamation)

Housing in Toyon, open only to government employees, filled quite rapidly as government inspectors and other personnel arrived from Grand Coulee, Parker and Boulder Dams. The opening of Toyon in late 1938 produced a flood of requests for additional housing.[19] The Bureau, however, hesitated with further construction until 1939 hoping to ascertain its full needs. In the course of the next few years the Bureau constructed several new homes on vacant lots. This proved inadequate, and for a number of years dozens of newly reassigned government men and their families rented homes in the boomtown areas. Waiting lists were established for housing in Toyon, which was eagerly sought because of the superior home construction and excellent utilities.

Services in Toyon paled in comparison to Boulder City. Whereas the latter, built as a model city, boasted a variety of commercial establishments offering both partial and full services. None of these services existed at Toyon. There was no camp market or commissary, no public gas station (gas was available for government vehicles on official business only), no recreation hall (although the government did turn the old Seaman's farmhouse into a community hall), or any of the dozens of services that many of the government workers had seen regularly at Boulder City.[20]

The converted Seaman's Ranch home provided a place for Toyon residents to relax and entertain. As shown above, it served also as a day-care center (Bureau of Reclamation).

As an unincorporated area of Shasta County, Toyon received police services from the Shasta County Sheriff's Department. However, except for occasional minor family squabbles, the county patrol cars rarely appeared on Toyon's streets. One lone red fire engine, housed in the community garage and manned by three part-time government men, provided fire protection for the new community.

31

The population of Toyon fluctuated between 800 and 1000, with 250 single men living in the dormitories and the balance housed in duplexes and single family homes. Social activities at Toyon for single men focused on the Bachelor's Club. However, this "club" limited its activities to offering breakfast and dinner meals prepared daily by a hired cook, Helen McDowell.

The converted Seaman's ranch house provided the citizens of Toyon with a community activity center. The two-story remodeled structure offered residents, usually women and children, a relaxed environment. Here government workers and their families celebrated holidays and other special occasions, usually formal and informal dinners. Oftentimes a spring or summer barbecue would be held outside on the grounds surrounding the center. Toyon residents invited guests from the contractor's camp and the boomtowns to many of these events.[21] Some of the men formed a baseball team and represented the Bureau in games played against other local teams, particularly boomtown teams. However, for the most part, Toyon men had little time for socializing as their work on the dam occupied most of their waking hours. The women and children of Toyon socialized much more than the men. Toyon women did have a few informal social clubs, where meetings moved from home to home. Many of them shopped and visited in the boomtowns or Redding on a regular basis and therefore joined and participated in many of the social groups formed in those areas.

Toyon School (Bureau of Reclamation)

The children of Toyon attended Toyon Elementary School. It was built collectively by Bureau personnel, Pacific Constructors men and boomtown workers. Within days of its opening, Toyon School filled to capacity, and shortly thereafter became swamped as students arrived daily. Matt Rumboltz, the first and longtime principal of Toyon school, recalled classrooms of forty, fifty, sixty, sometimes seventy students.[22]

Through most of the early years, 1938-1945, Toyon residents relied on Redding more than the nearby boomtowns for their shopping, entertainment, and general socializing. Single government workers preferred the bars, saloons, and "cathouses" of California Street in Redding to the smaller, more congested "fist houses" strung along boomtown's main drag, Shasta Dam Blvd.[23] Social bias appears to have had little to do with the Redding over boomtown preference. Stores in Redding offered greater variety and usually better quality items, particularly clothing and furniture.

Residents living in Toyon enjoyed wide-paved streets, sewers and help with landscaping (Bureau of Reclamation).

The physical appearance of Toyon showed signs of greenbelt planning. Wide paved roads separated nicely landscaped yards and homes. The town was surrounded by a permanent greenbelt insulating the community from the noisier boomtowns--Summit City (west) and Central

33

Valley and Project City (east). The landscaping at Toyon, like Coulee Dam (the government camp at Grand Coulee Dam), provided a garden-like setting. Strict regulations at Boulder City dictated that lawns, shrubs, and flowers must be well maintained by residents. Bureau of Reclamation representatives fined any who allowed their residences or businesses to lapse in upkeep. For New Deal Bureau supervisors, image was important, and hundreds, later thousands, of visitors toured Boulder City.

The standardized same-income lifestyle evident in Toyon had appeared earlier at Grand Coulee Dam. Bureau representatives designed the government town of Coulee Dam, and like Toyon, ran the community. The Bureau decided everything from the color of homes to landscaping and even the speed limit on roads.[24]

The physical layout of Toyon fits nicely into the general concepts of the New Deal greenbelt communities as analyzed by James Dahir in Greendale Comes of Age. Dahir contended that four main goals of the greenbelt planning committee included limiting the growth of the town itself, defining boundaries that would preserve identity, preventing encroachment by other towns, and providing a pervasive country setting.[25] In all these areas, the construction and running of Toyon appeared to follow suit. The growth of Toyon, limited from the beginning, forced many government personnel to look for housing elsewhere, usually in the boomtowns located nearby. In fact, growth remained severely limited in Toyon throughout War II. The main road, Shasta Dam Boulevard, defined the limits of the town to the south, while the hills to the north and adjacent greenbelt zones to the east and west successfully buffered the town from encroachment and added to the natural setting.

Important differences existed between the greenbelt communities of the New Deal and the dam boomtowns. First, private ownership of homes was forbidden. All government employees rented or leased their dwellings in Toyon. Dahir argued that, from the beginning, New Deal policies included the eventual transition of home ownership from public to private. This process took considerable time however, and Greendale residents did not acquire private ownership options until 1952.[26] Second, the greenbelt communities provided no industrial employment opportunities. Instead, the towns had been located on the outskirts of major cities in the hopes that greenbelt residents would successfully secure urban jobs. Toyon, on the other hand, existed exclusively to house government workers building Shasta Dam.

Bureau of Reclamation engineers and staff gathered at Toyon (Bureau of Reclamation)

In addition to the above mentioned differences Toyon did not allow commercial establishments or cultural structures such as schools or churches. All the greenbelt communities contained preplanned commercial centers and well-placed churches of several denominations. Greendale alone boasted three formal churches in its early history, reaching six established structures in later years.[27] Likewise, Greendale from the outset planned high schools, a large intermediate school and several elementary schools to cover the educational requirements of a new town.[28] Toyon contained no school. Toyon School was built on federal land a short distance away, but the funds for constructing the building came from Pacific Constructors Inc., the contracting firm responsible for building Shasta Dam. Greendale's Village Center contained many privately owned businesses that functioned under the same kind of rules that regulated Boulder City entrepreneurs. Opportunities were necessarily restricted, as planners considered commercial sprawl more damaging than residential expansion. Government officials at Toyon, like its sister dam town at Grand Coulee, refused to issue any commercial permits, thus opening the door for numerous boomtown business owners to exploit the economic opportunities of providing goods and services to dam workers.

Duplex homes offered parking in-between the living quarters (Bureau of Reclamation).

Architecturally, the greenbelt government homes displayed much greater varieties of interior and exterior designs than did any of the dam towns. In Greendale, planners selected fourteen different basic styles and drew in minor variations within these to prevent presenting a manufactured community.[29] Home designs in Toyon varied only in terms of number of bedrooms offered and location of interior partitions.

One of the stark differences between Toyon and the model greenbelt cities occurred in the way in which prospective residents were selected. Toyon's newly hired government employees simply waited the necessary time period, sometimes as long as six months, for a vacancy to occur in either the duplexes or the single family homes. Some preference was given to higher-level management personnel. However, many of them preferred to live in Redding and commute to work. The greenbelt cities posed a stark contrast. The Resettlement Administration, set up an intricate interview and screening procedure that frustrated and eliminated many applicants. Emphasis at first focused on lower income families, mostly displaced and unemployed—but skilled workers and their families predominated later. The resettlement communities, composed of both the greenbelt cities and numerous rural subsistence farms, struggled as newly arrived residents found it difficult to obtain employment and pay for their higher standard of living.[30] This problem pervaded almost all the established experiments. Paul

Conklin in his book on New Deal community planning illustrated the problem arguing that the model community at Gee's Bend, Alabama needed the full and ongoing support of federal assistance, including food and clothing. This support kept the community viable. Placed in new homes near their old cotton farms, the apparent success of the new community proved to be merely a facade.[31]

Government subsidies in the field of medical and health services, pioneered by the Resettlement Administration in its community program, also surfaced at Toyon. The overall government plan for medical assistance for model community residents took effect in 1936. This plan happened, a year and a half before Toyon's medical coverage became operative. These early attempts at government sponsored group medical plans initiated the ongoing government involvement in health care benefits for its citizens.[32] The Resettlement Administration's plan and the Bureau of Reclamation's concept appear quite similar. The client paid a small monthly fee ($2.00) that went into a group fund. An active member of the group could use the local medical facilities at any time and coverage included most illnesses. While membership remained at the voluntary level most, if not all, residents took advantage of the coverage. Every employee of Toyon participated. Medical coverage did not extend to the worker's family dependents. However, with the exception of obstetrics and tuberculosis, medical costs at the government sponsored hospital remained reasonable.

Workers leveling the driveway and sidewalks on the single family homes in Toyon (Bureau of Reclamation).

View of Toyon nearing completion in 1938. Plans called for keeping many of the Digger pine trees growing in the area (Bureau of Reclamation).

Chapter 4
Shasta Dam Village (Contractor's Camp)

Like other previous dam contractors, Pacific Constructors Inc. (PCI), the successful company to bid for the Shasta Dam job, selected a location for the new town as close to the work site as was feasible. This was accomplished under the leadership of veteran dam builder Frank Crowe. Crowe laid out a functional company town plan. The administrative offices and supply shops sat next to dormitory-type living quarters (for single men) and the mess hall. Family homes usually clustered some distance away.[1]

Many company towns proudly pointed to their well-planned rectangular shaped grid plan. PCI however, forced to grapple with local hilly terrain, began construction in late 1938 with little concern for geometric conformity. The streets, as they were cut-in, followed natural hillside contours.[2] Street names denoted clusters of workers who had shared earlier job experiences: Boulder Dam Avenue constituted the largest gathering, while representatives from Parker Dam, Bonneville Dam, Ft. Peck Dam, Grand Coulee Dam, the All-American Canal, and other smaller projects all had names given to streets.

First to be erected, as was true in most company towns, was the dormitory and mess hall. Construction of the H-shaped dormitory and the large U-shaped mess hall, occurred in September of 1938. The dorm, originally designed to hold 172 single-men, later underwent modification to shelter 265 mostly single workers.[3] The rooms inside, provided adequate though austere environments, with conformity the rule rather than the exception. There existed no status or seniority-based hierarchy to room assignments for location. With available space exhausted, company workers found housing in one of the quickly rising boomtowns nearby.

In rapid succession PCI completed the tiny community, erecting offices, shops, another dormitory for office personnel, a well-stocked monopolistic general store, an often-visited and much-liked coffee shop, a cavernous recreation hall complete with pool and card tables, a well-equipped fire station, and an excellent hospital. By the end of 1938, 131 single-family homes had also been completed and occupied. These newly finished structures were mass-produced with standardized construction.

Pine wood exteriors and composition interior walls provided little relief from the scorching north valley summers and the biting-cold winters. Homeowners however did enjoy electric cooking stoves and water heaters. Some used oil heating stoves and struggled to normalize interior winter temperatures. Six months later rugged and inventive dam pioneers rigged home-made "swamp coolers" in an attempt to survive weeks of 100 degree summer temperatures.[4]

Single family home going up at Shasta Dam Village. A long waiting list quickly developed as workers and their families desired this quality construction (Bureau of Reclamation).

Most floor plans revealed four rooms including one bedroom, a kitchen, living room, and a bathroom. A limited number of larger homes became available to allow for additional bedrooms. Higher level PCI employees, including foremen and managers, usually secured these homes. Occasionally, lower level personnel moved into larger homes.[5] Most people lived in the one-bedroom model, complaining little about the tight accommodations. They were happy to have a "roof over their head."[6]

James Allen in his book *The Company Town in the American West* related the traditional style of company town homes as having a kitchen, living room, one or two bedrooms, and a bath. Some residents added a screened porch to double as an extra sleeping area.[7] This follows the type of construction utilized at Shasta Dam Village and points to the fact that on the whole, construction workers were indeed fortunate to secure this compact, yet adequate, housing. Allen also noted the somewhat unusual possibility of permitting individual employees to build their own shelters within the boundaries of the company town. This did not happen at the Shasta site. First, Frank Crowe had experienced life in many dam construction camps and he knew that company housing usually was superior and more desirable than individually erected structures that regularly took the shape of squatter shacks.[8] Second, steep topography limited building sites. Moreover, Shasta Dam had already received national attention, as had Hoover and Grand Coulee Dams, and the Bureau of Reclamation insisted that housing at Shasta Dam Village and at its own town of Toyon reaffirm, in a positive manner, the goals of the New Deal—decent housing for government workers. The final determinant centered on the fact that the job at Shasta would take years to complete and that living conditions needed to be stable to enhance morale and worker productivity.

By the end of 1938, dozens of single-family homes dotted a lower hill near the construction site (Bureau of Reclamation).

Certainly, the housing at Shasta Dam Village and Toyon proved superior in both materials used and utilities offered, than any seen in the nearby commercial boomtowns. Shasta Dam Village provided residents with community water, sewerage, full electric service, and telephone service. As far back as 1912, the Spring Canyon Coal Company helped set a precedent for western company towns by establishing a policy of providing improved housing conditions, including water, sewerage, and "substantially constructed" homes.[9]

The single men's dormitory at Shasta Dam Village is nearing completion in this photograph. Notice the sparse vegetation in the nearby hills. This denudation occurred in early decades from the copper smelting fumes.

Company officials did not encourage residents to alter their homes. Companies painted all homes the same color, insisted on conformity in landscaping, and disapproved requests to alter the physical structure of the house itself, such as adding a bedroom or expanding the living room. Allen noted that this policy of conformity changed during the middle years of the twentieth century toward a more liberalized attitude. The lumber town at McCloud, California, once presented row after row of homes painted a uniform gray. By 1950 multi-colored dwellings appeared, although residents still had no decision as to which color their house would be.[10]

Signs of conformity appeared at Shasta Dam Village. Here home construction and paint colors were identical throughout the town. In previous jobs of short duration this did not appear to present a problem for most residents. However, the long-duration dam projects marooned workers in shelters that proved devoid of their personal touch. Was this a significant problem to the residents? The answer appears to be, no. Residents stated that they appreciated this type of uniform housing because they had it much better than their counterparts struggling to build homes in the boomtowns.

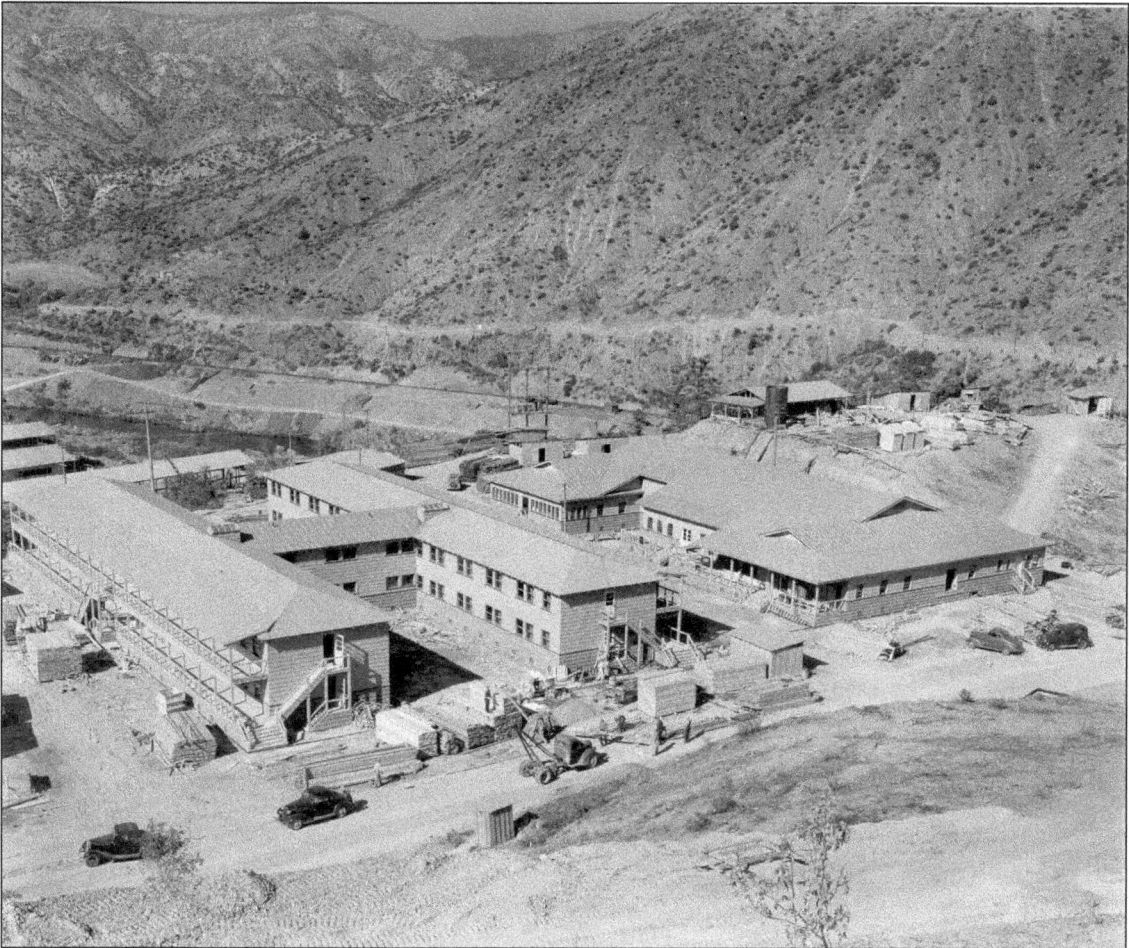

The Mess Hall, shown here to the right of the dormitory, provided seating for hundreds of workers at one time and included a "game room" with pool tables (Bureau of Reclamation).

Allen argued that company towns, for the most part, charged reasonably low rents and provided good services. He added that this was necessary to induce hesitant workers to live in isolated and primitive areas."[11] With the average starting salary at $.99 an hour (by November of 1944 wages rose to $1.60), Shasta Dam workers earned approximately

$48.00 a week of which they paid $9.00 a week in rent. The rental fee, then, worked out to be twenty-five percent of their total gross pay, reasonable even by today's standards. Company officials deducted all rent payments directly from the worker's paychecks.

Housing conformity is as much perception as it is reality, and at Shasta Dam Village the perception noted by visitors centered on appearances. Yet, numerous village residents displayed their individuality through landscaping, vegetable gardens, and even room additions. The usual addition, which did not require a permit or permission to pursue, involved walling-in part or all, of the screened porch. Most often the new room would serve as an extra bedroom. This type of nonconformity became quite popular because there would be no increase in the rental fee for additions.[12]

The mess hall, commissary, and recreation hall centralized social life in Shasta Dam Village. Workers purchased weekly meal tickets that offered up to four healthy, well-prepared meals. Government personnel living in Toyon and dam workers living in the boomtowns often purchased meal tickets, once word spread of how good the food was, and much socializing went on here. Discussions, of course, centered on job talk and what the next shift might bring. Workers also planned off-work activities, such as movies, shopping, dinners with friends, sporting recreation—particularly fishing, and future work plans.[13] The commissary, open to government and boomtown residents sold first-rate merchandise especially groceries at reasonable rates. Until the Safeway store opened in Central Valley, most workers and their families purchased necessary food items, and some dry goods from the commissary. Recreation hall entertainment limited workers to pool tables and card tables (usually penny-ante poker). Sometimes the games, particularly after payday evolved into intense competition as poker-faced concrete spreaders challenged iron-willed truck drivers. Brash tempers were calmed by stern-faced Pat Unger, supervisor of the mess hall-commissary-recreation hall-dormitory complex. Unger's heady personality preempted suggestive comments from erupting into full-blown fist-flying brawls.[14]

Allen commented that almost every company town before 1940 stocked and ran at least one company store. The idea was to serve the workers, but more often than not, the lone commissary proved self-serving, a further extension of control over the workers. In fact, some companies demanded that workers purchase all their necessary supplies from the company store, which, of course, regulated prices and profits. At Sunnyside, Utah, the Utah Fuel Company terminated any employee caught "patronizing the other stores for things that could be obtained at much higher prices in the company store." At Shasta Dam Village, no competition existed for the company store.[15] However, residents regularly patronized other boomtown stores or shops in Redding when items were not obtainable at the commissary.[16] Allen argued that, with respect to prices and the quality of merchandise, company stores had a reputation for top grades of meat and produce as well as high quality clothing items, and that prices charged for merchandise ran slightly higher than most nearby commercial establishments.[17] The argument of company store domination centered around the necessity of providing good quality inventories along with moderate prices as an incentive to keep good workers on the job. The situation at Shasta Dam revealed general approval of the quality of items and of the prices charged. Most workers residing at the camp and their wives shopped regularly and almost exclusively at the company store.

The twenty bed air-conditioned hospital built by Pacific Constructors for the Shasta Dam job, when finished, was the best equipped hospital north of Sacramento. The hospital staff included two doctors, twelve nurses—half of them males and an X-ray laboratory technician. Dr. John Kirkpatrick, a competent physician and an able administrator, supervised the running of the hospital. His stay at the dam site lasted the entire length of the six-year period. Kirkpatrick insisted on absolutely clean rooms and ultra- sanitary conditions.

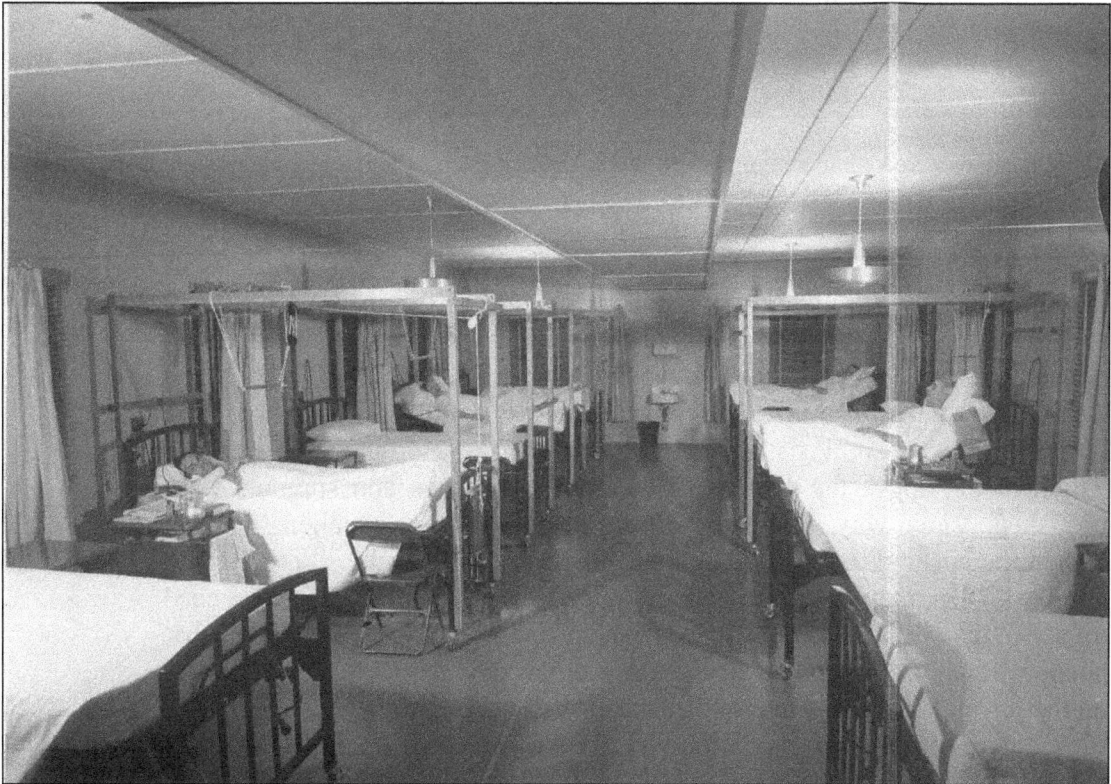

Word spread quickly to nearby towns, including, that the hospital at Shasta Dam Village contained some of the most advanced medical equipment and facilities, north of Sacramento (Bureau of Reclamation).

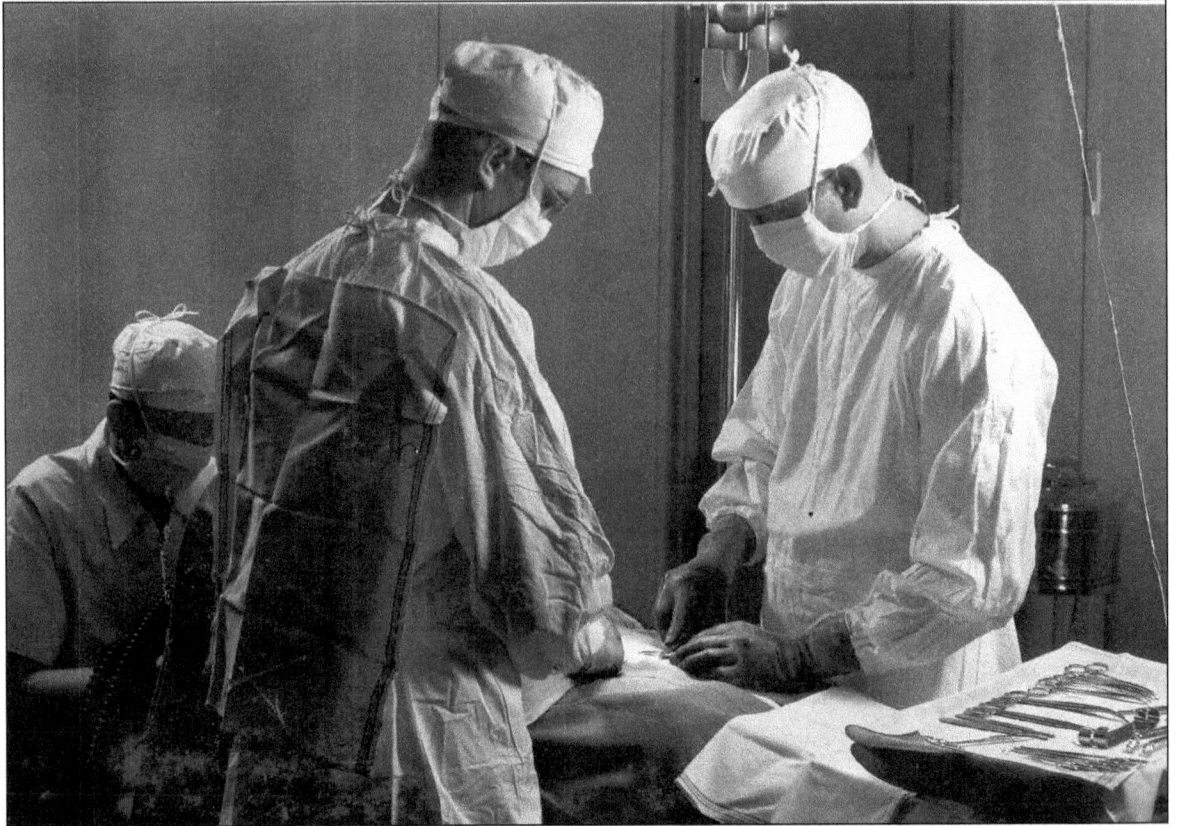

While fatalities were kept to a minimum at Shasta Dam, accidents did happen and prompt medical attention was always available (Bureau of Reclamation).

The hospital served all workers at Shasta Dam, not just residents of the company town. A workman could participate in the medical program, and almost all did, for the reasonable fee of two dollars a month. PCI opened medical coverage to allow dependents on the subsidized plan. For a small fee, a wife or child could receive medical care in all cases except obstetrics and tuberculosis.[18] There was no limit to the number of times a patient could apply for dispensary care, and all drugs and supplies were furnished. Viola May, boomtown resident, implied that excellent medical care at the hospital improved employer-employee relationships, lowered the number of lost man-hours, in general helped the dam construction proceed on schedule.[19] Shasta Dam Village resident George Van Eaton added that hospital benefits encouraged workers in the boomtowns, particularly, to stay on the job and enjoy community life more.[20]

Company towns have a long tradition of making concerted efforts to provide adequate school facilities for their workers' children. Many companies understood that school buildings would also serve as community centers, and Parent Teachers Associations linked families together as school functions increased. Some companies initially would build the school and hire a teacher, while more often the company would work with the local county board of education. A company representative would then serve on the board. Allen argued that this system sometimes led to company controlled school boards, as company money and influence permeated the county.[21] When the company moved on to other jobs, the school building would be sold to the school district.

As the summer of 1938 progressed it became obvious that some sort of school facilities would be needed. In addition to the many children already in residence at Shasta Dam Village and Toyon there were untold scores more hiding in the bush around the many squatter camps. The original contract between the Bureau of Reclamation and PCI required the company to make arrangements for the education of the workers' children, and PCI Superintendent Frank Crowe, needed only to build a modest school house on the property at Shasta Dam. This would have left scores of nervous and anxious children living in the commercial boomtowns without a school. Fortunately, Shasta County Superintendent of Schools, Macie Montgomery, reviewed the demographic problem of finding facilities for four to five hundred boomtown children, and persuaded Crowe to build the school on federal land near Summit City, next to the government town of Toyon. Additionally, PCI would provide two school busses, one to haul children from Shasta Dam Village, Toyon, and the boomtowns to the new elementary school. The other bus operated by Shasta Union High School, would transport the older students to Shasta High School in Redding.[22]

The school project became a joint project with PCI supplying most of the materials and labor. However, the Bureau of Reclamation provided and installed the necessary water pipes. They also supplied a huge amount of fence material, which when delivered, was erected by the older school boys under adult supervision.[23] County school personnel brought over as many desks as they could spare and unpacked boxes of books and school material. The whole venture provided an excellent example of company and community cooperation rarely seen in today's highly structured system of school administration and finance.

Company towns historically have supported and even encouraged their workers to participate in religious activities. If the work site was situated close to an already existing community with churches, the company would do little except to encourage attendance. However, many western companies agreed to build churches and staff them with ministers. When the town was too small to realize the need for a separate church structure, religious services would be held in halls or schools. In at least one lumber town the company allowed the part-time minister to work in the mill.[24]

Numerous examples of company supported churches abound in the West. The Union Pacific Coal Company, located a town at Hanna,

Wyoming, quickly offered land and materials for the building of a Methodist-Episcopal church in 1891. In McCloud, California, the McCloud River Lumber Company built the local community church, furnished a home for the minister, and paid him a small stipend. Company administrators of the Phelps Dodge Corporation in Dawson, New Mexico, found a home for the newly arrived Protestant minister, and provided "other subsidies."[25] Discrimination by companies favoring one religious group over another appears to be rare in Western company town history. At McCloud, the company contributed in one way or another to the building of the Baptist, Catholic, Episcopal, and Mt. Zion Baptist (Black) churches.

In this photograph, a truckload of workers begin a new shift, departing from their residence at the Village (Bureau of Reclamation).

Shasta Dam Village contained no church or even offered religious services. There had been no particular demand by the workers and with the building of two churches in the boomtowns, those inclined to attend services drove into Central Valley or Redding.[26] This lack of company leadership in building a company supported church does not appear too

48

unusual when considering past experiences at Hoover and Grand Coulee Dams. Six Companies, the contractor at Hoover Dam, would have nothing to do with building a church, hiring a minister, or even suggesting church participation. Workers of varying religions formed community church groups and raised the money to erect their own establishments of worship.

Thomas E. ("Parson Tom") Stevenson, a Presbyterian minister from Burbank, California spewed forth his hell-fire and damnation sermons from the River Camp mess hail. From here Parson Tom drew large crowds in Boulder City, enough to afford construction of the impressive Grace Community Church.[27] Shortly, Catholic workers erected St. Andrew's Church under the leadership of Father Hogan. By the end of 1932, two more churches, one a Mormon place of worship, had been completed. The same situation existed in Grand Coulee, where government and company administrators appeared reluctant to involve themselves in church building. Religiously inclined workers formed groups in the adjacent boomtowns and erected their own churches.

While the neophyte construction companies at each of the dam projects were sensitive to the religious needs of their numerous employees, they shied away from any active involvement. The Bureau of Reclamation also revealed surprisingly little interest in church raising and subsequent religious functions. No official government policy statement can be found concerning government attitudes, regulations, and or involvement towards religion and church building within the realm of government sponsored or associated community building.

The ethnic composition of Shasta Dam Village can be described quite simply: all white. A few Mexicans, blacks, and dozens of local Indians worked on Shasta Dam, but none resided in the village. Neither did they live in Toyon, the government town. Instead most lived in and around Redding, with only a handful reported to have "homes" in the boomtowns. Allen reported that company towns never have had a good record of desegregating their communities. He reported separate living arrangements in the majority of western company towns even on up through the 1960s.[28] In at least one fully documented case, a western company town in Gamerco, New Mexico planned its town with separate resident quarters for the large number of Mexican and Indian workers, rationalizing that the Mexicans "prefer to live in more or less segregated quarters," and "the Navajos build their own 'hoogans' and the solution of their housing problems does not rest on the mine owner."[29]

One black man did work at the Shasta Dam Village site. He labored as a janitor in the auto shop, but lived in Redding. Village residents stated that he was nicknamed "whitey" and was an easygoing good-hearted man. He was not seen socializing with any of the village workers.[30]

Phi Delta Kappa college graduate engineers lived alongside company construction "stiffs" at the village. Climbing the company ladder involved laboring for years within one of the sub-companies of PCI. Workers, especially those that developed cordial relationships with higher level company personnel, along with a proven work record, moved into foremen and management positions. Many men in the supervisor capacity had earned their rank through years of dedicated service to the "old man"— general superintendent Frank Crowe and almost all of the company residents boasted of previous work experience on Hoover, Parker, Ft. Peck, or Grand Coulee Dams.

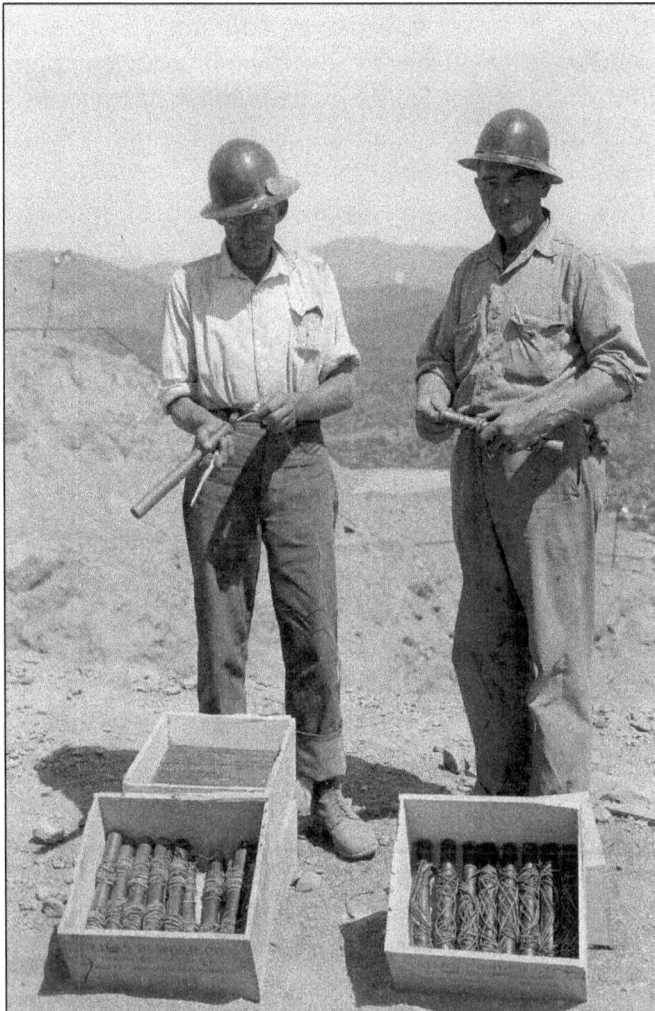

Workers from a wide background of education and employment experience labored together at the dam site. Here the engineer (left) is reviewing the priming procedure for the explosives with his assistant (Bureau of Reclamation).

Much respect would be given to men who were "without benefit of school diplomas," but, who had proven their worth on other dam projects. Despite the educational discrepancies of company workers in residence at Shasta Dam Village, social mixing was everywhere obvious and continued throughout the building years with congeniality and enthusiasm.[31]

Residents of Shasta Dam Village noted that life in general for them varied little from that of any other typical American small town community. Entertainment of the homemade variety reigned supreme. Informal get-togethers, usually dinner, cards, and conversation, provided a Saturday or Sunday evening's social activity. News and gossip traveled rapidly from one home to another or from dorm room to dorm room.

Workers finishing their shift climb on the commute trucks and prepare to head back to the dormitories or the boomtowns (Bureau of Reclamation).

Allen contended that early to mid-twentieth century company towns found themselves heavily involved in the social affairs of their employees. Not only did the company build and maintain recreational facilities for its employees, but they also, to a great extent, insisted on participation at company sponsored events.[32] This did not happen at Shasta. There were few social events at Shasta Dam Village, although many residents attended other social activities, such as dinners, ice cream socials, awards ceremonies, at Toyon and in the boomtowns. It appears that PCI firmly believed in a "hands off" social policy. The company did allow the posting of private social events in the commissary and recreation hall. Bridge clubs drew enthusiastic groups of card players on Friday and Saturday evenings and a women's book club gathered to talk about the latest local and international news, as well as information on interesting literature.[33]

PCI did sponsor a local baseball team that engaged in hard- hitting slugfests against Redding and boomtown teams. Prior to the weekly bouts, anxious dam workers debated the attributes and weaknesses of opposing teams, and at times ventured small bets. Bowling too, aroused enthusiastic responses from village workers. A company team, organized by the workers, squared off against the best competition from Redding and the main boomtown, Central Valley.[34]

One social activity that played an important role later in enticing the dam workers to stay on in the Shasta Dam area involved the local environment. When workers discovered that Clear Creek, Hat Creek, and other tributaries of the Sacramento River, had once given up substantial amounts of gold dust and nuggets, they spent their days off gold panning, and in some cases dredging for the "yellow stuff." Families and groups of families could be seen picnicking by the nearby lakes and streams, particularly on Sundays. Fishing and hunting inspired many workers to spend a considerable amount of their free time discovering the geography of Shasta County.

Although residents at Shasta Dam Village realized that their job and homes belonged to the company, they felt little of the traditional condescending attitude of paternalism. Information obtained from written questionnaires and oral interviews suggest that dam workers appreciated job opportunities and homes in the village, and they recalled no blatant abuses to their rights or loss of personal liberties. To some extent, they had grown to accept the conditions of employment, and considering the difficult times of the late Depression years, one can understand their forthright defense of company life.

The rules and regulations allowed for much leeway, and residents took advantage of this opportunity constantly. Company home interiors, landscaping, socializing, and off-work dress all displayed examples of individual initiative and desires. Residents in the single-family section of

Shasta Dam Village report that Meritt Butler, the person in charge of the structures, busied himself with maintenance problems. He was congenial and easy to get along with.[35]

The main administration building at Shasta Dam Village, shown here, housed Pacific Constructor's engineers and office staff (Bureau of Reclamation).

One of the best paying jobs at the Shasta Dam construction site focused on operating heavy equipment, such as the bulldozer (above) and pickup shovels (below) (Bureau of Reclamation).

Many of the construction jobs proved dangerous and workers needed to concentrate for long periods of time. The jack-hammer operator shown above is drilling the blasting holes for explosive charges. Men complained of ongoing arm and shoulder problems from the ongoing vibration of the jack-hammer (Bureau of Reclamation).

Chapter 5
The Boomtowns: Stores and Businesses

The Shasta Dam area boomtowns, Central Valley, Project City, and Summit City follow the sector model of urban development as explained out by Homer Hoyt, a land economist. Using data collected from over 100 cities, Hoyt suggested that once similar commercial development formed around a community nucleus, growth would occur along lines of established arterial flow, thus forming outward moving sectors of development.[1] Hoyt's investigation concluded that boomtown growth centered around zones of one or more major transportation avenues, linking already existing urbanized areas to newly forming boomtowns.

The boomtowns were located some seven miles north of the city of Redding, and two miles from Shasta Dam. By late 1938 and early 1939 the two main avenues of access to the dam site from Redding had been well laid out. Branching off in a westerly direction, the newly graded and sealed Grand Coulee Blvd. (later Shasta Dam Blvd.), bristled with the reflections of hundreds of automobiles moving daily to and from the dam site. The old Kennett Road that had joined Redding with the recently abandoned copper smelting town of Kennett, blossomed with new life as Bureau authorities graded, widened and graveled.

The juxtaposition of squatter camps to these two main arteries presaged urban development and fulfilled Hoyt's prediction of coalescence along lines of least resistance and greatest resident opportunity (i.e. access to transportation avenues linking already existing or newly located job sources). The main boomtown area nucleated along both sides of Grand Coulee Blvd. and the northern section of Kennett Road.[2]

Speculation increased with the public announcement of the building of Shasta Dam. Get-rich-quick schemes abounded, usually centering around land purchasing and subdividing home lots. As far south as Buckeye, an already existing tiny bedroom community, developers rushed to advertise prime building locations in close proximity to the dam construction site. By February of 1939, little Buckeye expanded to include dozens of new homes, numerous parcels with trailers parked on them, a new post office, a real estate office, and even a library. For those seeking only temporary housing, scores of rental cabins dotted the landscape.[3] Meanwhile, a half a mile to the north on Kennett Road slumbering Newtown, previously consisting of a few small isolated farmsteads, spawned only a handful of new homes and no commercial business. Expecting a tremendous boom, land in and around Buckeye and Newtown quickly sold. However, with the realization that Kennett Road would not be paved for several years and that it was destined to be employed more for transporting heavy equipment between Redding and the dam site, speculation fizzled by late 1939. The real boomtown activity appeared reserved for locations flanking Grand Coulee Blvd.[4]

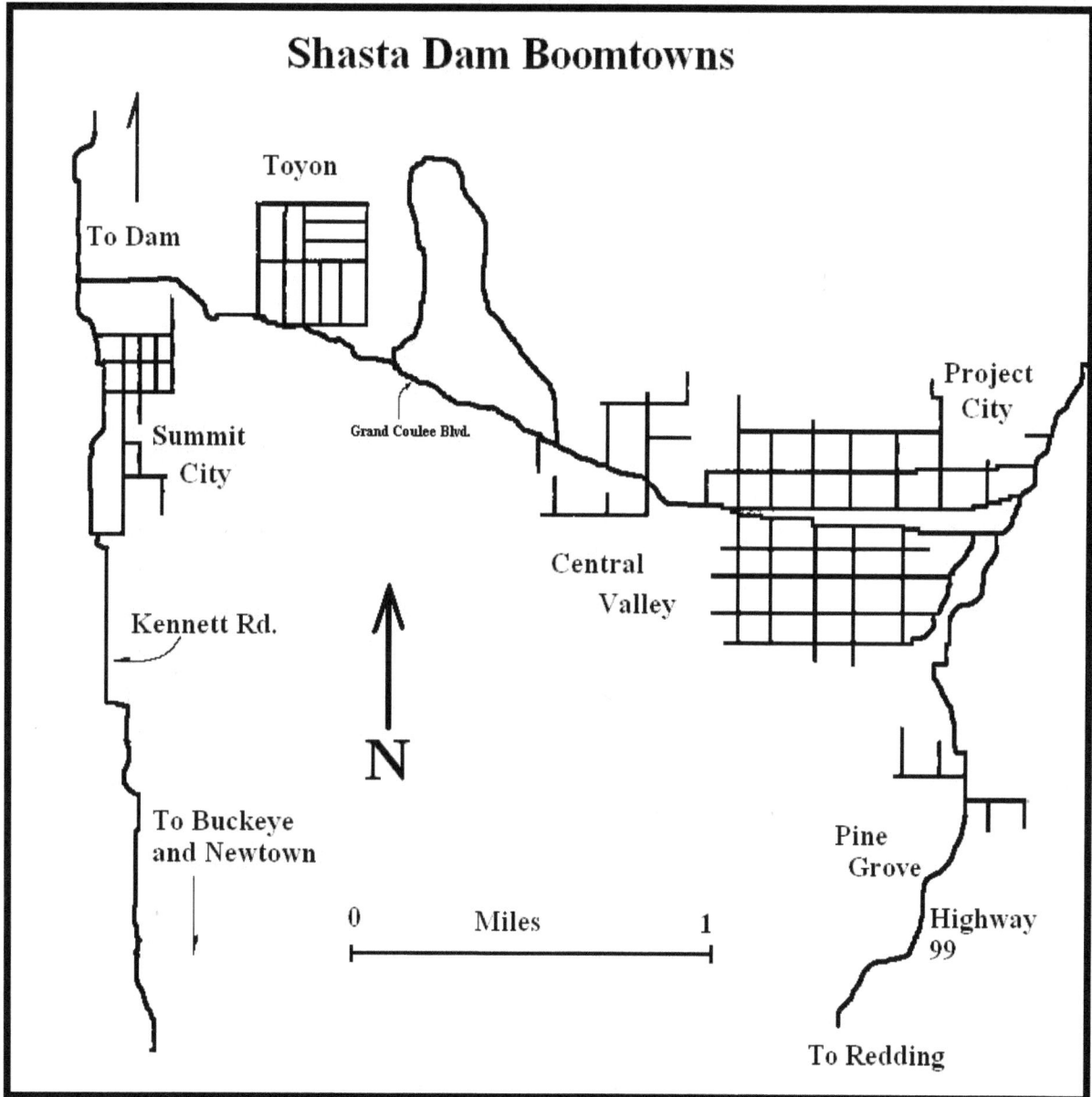

Shasta Dam Boomtowns

Toyon

To Dam

Project City

Summit City

Grand Coulee Blvd.

Kennett Rd.

Central Valley

N

To Buckeye and Newtown

Pine Grove

Highway 99

0 Miles 1

To Redding

More promising was Charles Akard's idea of locating a new town along either side of U.S. Highway 99. With the name Pine Grove and oversized lots, Akard hoped to lure recently arrived Boulder and Parker Dam ex-workers, more at home with small company housing and searing-hot desert sands, into buying his lots. After abortive attempts to land a school and a post office, Akard had to settle with selling some of his residential property.[5]

The main boomtown activity, strung out along either side of Grand Coulee Blvd., extended from U.S. Highway 99 west three miles to the junction of the Kennett/Buckeye Road. Except for a small portion of federal land near Toyon, commercial and residential buildings sprang forth at a dizzying pace. Beginning in late 1937 and continuing strong until mid-1939, scores of businesses opened and hundreds of residences appeared. Many long-time Shasta County residents remember the boomtown area before all the activity as nothing more than "great jack-rabbit country" or "two farmsteads and a dirt road."[6] Wild berry picking had been the main attraction for both area residents and visitors.

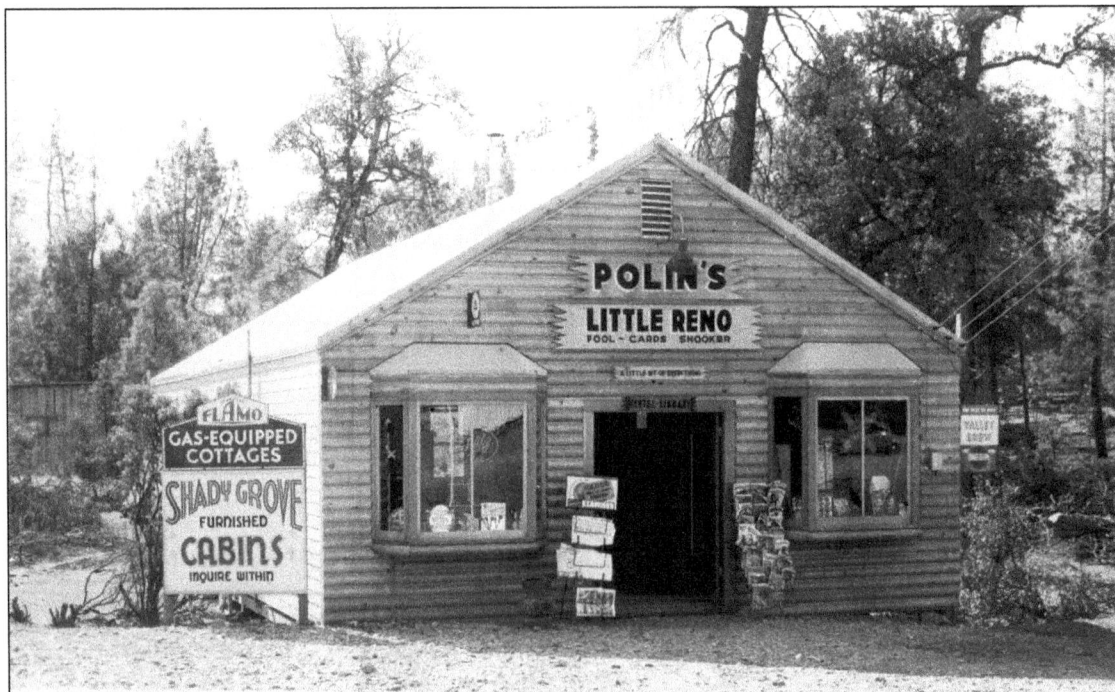

A favorite for just about everyone in the boomtown area, Polin's Little Reno drew dam workers for pool, cards, and snooker. Notice the sign to the left advertising "gas-equipped cottages" for newly arrived job hopefuls (Shasta Historical Society).

Speculation focused on two "get-rich-quick" schemes. The first method involved the age-old system of buying up large quantities of cheap

58

land in and around the proposed area of activity. At first, this proved difficult as it was not clear how much land the Bureau of Reclamation would itself purchase. When it became obvious that land adjacent the Sacramento River would be held as federal property, land speculators, such as J. C. Tibbitts of Redding, concentrated their efforts around the quickly developing squatter camps already buzzing with activity along the recently cut and graded Shasta Dam Blvd. The other method of money-making, also typical in western boomtown history, involved selling goods and services to the thousands of anxiously awaiting dam workers.[7] Marion Allen, a dam worker at both Boulder and Shasta Dams, recalled that when he first arrived in Boulder City, early in the project (1934), there were many would-be entrepreneurs trying to "separate the dam workers from their money."[8] Frank Lyman, an editor for the San Francisco Examiner on assignment at the proposed Shasta Dam site in 1938, noted considerable business activity. He added that additional economic opportunity would result from recreational based businesses, once the dam was completed and the reservoir filled.[9]

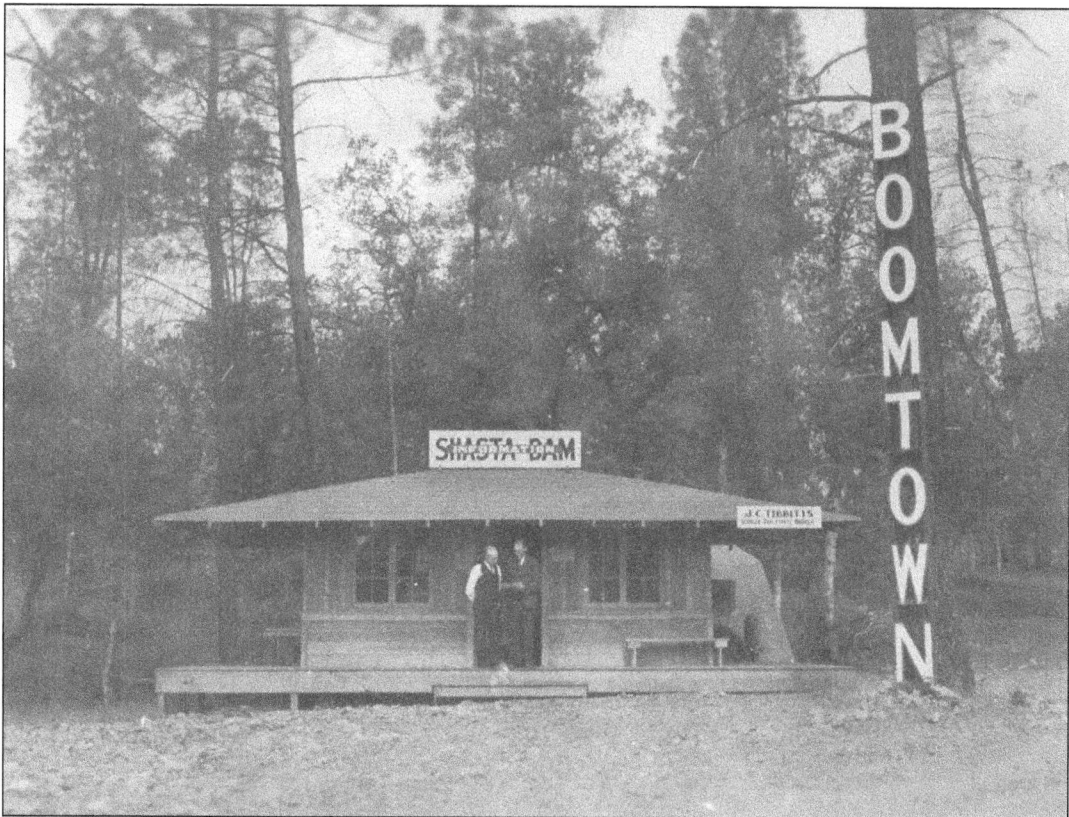

Realtor Jonathan Tibbitts (left) discussing real estate options with a would-be buyer. The boomtown tree sign became a famous landmark during the first years of development (Shasta Historical Society).

An early occupant and resident throughout much of the boomtown period, educator Matt Rumboltz, wrote that a "sort of stringtown" extended along Shasta Dam Blvd. from Highway U.S. 99 to the Kennett/Buckeye Road.[10] Most of the early businesses tended to be service oriented. These included pool halls, saloons, restaurants, service stations, a theatre, a skating rink, and dance halls. Small grocery stores, a drug store, and various variety stores supplied local needs for everyday items. Liquor stores, prohibited by law from selling hard liquor within three miles of any government sponsored project, never materialized.

The three main boomtowns Central Valley, Project City, and Summit City all coalesced at about the same time. From the original squatter camps scattered about the vicinity of Toyon (government camp), Summit City quickly formed near the corner of the two main roads leading into the dam site.

Barbeque food was, and remains a favorite in Shasta County. The Southern Barbeque Restaurant, located in Summit City, offered a choice of beef and/or pork ribs. Hamburgers were also a favorite barbeque order (Shasta Historical Society).

As was typical of traditional boomtown experiences, the first commercial enterprises to spring up in Summit City catered to the eating and drinking demands of hard-working construction laborers, particularly government workers and their families isolated in Toyon. With the Bureau's decision to prohibit businesses from the federal reservation area, and the added directive that Toyon workers should take their meals at the contractor's mess hall in Shasta Dam Village, enterprising persons opened numerous beer halls, taverns, and restaurants. Charley's Candy and Lunches, The Round-Up (tavern), Superior Cafe, McCarthy's Cafe, and the Southern Barbecue were among the first businesses established in Summit City.[11]

When it became apparent, that the contractor's commissary could not provide the full range of dry goods necessary for workers and their families, commercial opportunities expanded in the area to include clothing, shoe shops, and variety stores. The 25' x 70' Phetteplace Variety Store opened by autumn of 1938, brought in customers from as far away as Redding, and prompted a local Redding newspaper to proclaim that lucrative business opportunities now existed in the dam area.[12]

Cafes such as this one in Central Valley proved popular with the dam workers and their families (Shasta Historical Society).

Redding merchants, sensing a chance for more profits, scrambled to extend their already existing services to the dam area. Mrs. Annie Amos opened a branch store of her highly successful Redding Bakery. Driving fresh donuts from Redding daily, entrepreneur Amos was an instant success in the Summit City area.[13] Local resident Joe Abplanalp invested hundreds of dollars to initiate his unique open-air barbecue pit restaurant. Specializing in large barbecue sandwiches and extra rich coffee, the

Southern Barbecue became a local favorite.[14] A few local builders, such as general contractor A. J. Hendricks, realized the need for immediate housing in Summit City and worked at a feverish pace to raise new dwellings and commercial buildings. Hendricks, who had moved from the San Joaquin Valley after visiting the area and seeing its commercial possibilities, himself invested in and built a large auto court consisting of twenty cottages, parking, restaurant, store, and laundry area. With an eye for improving the previous ramshackle squatter developments in the area, Hendricks strove to construct good quality housing, "I am building better houses than the average auto court in order to get away from the 'plain shacks' idea."[15]

Auto courts sprouted in the Summit City area throughout 1938. The courts themselves contained many of the commercial attributes of a small town, offering a general store, eatery, gas station, and dry goods. Asa Douthit and George Ayers opened one of the first auto courts, building eighteen cottages and parking spaces. In addition to the usual supporting stores, their popular confectionery business brought in many outside customers.[16] Another auto court developer E. R. Shields, from Bakersfield, realizing the need for comfortable low-cost temporary housing erected a well laid-out auto court featuring large cottages with "more than usual" open space between dwellings.[17]

Summit City's grew quickly in late 1938 and early 1939, with new stores opening up every month (Shasta Historical Society).

With P. G. & E. electricity installed over most of the Summit City area by the end of 1938, additional businesses opened their doors soon after. From Red Bluff came enterprising used car dealer Milton T. Morgan. Morgan surmised correctly that transportation would be needed by boomtown residents. Never believing in doing anything in a small way and calculating the auto needs of hundreds of workers, Milton gathered no less than sixty cars for his grand opening in December of 1938.[18] To service all these new cars, John DeLaGrange of San Francisco, pooled his resources together and opened a fully equipped AAA Garage.[19]

As December came to an end in 1938 business boomed, more job hopefuls poured into the Summit City area, and local business owners counted mostly profits. One large diner reported serving 400 dinners on a typical Sunday, with much of this business coming from Toyon.[20]

The man who contributed the most to promoting Summit City during the early boomtown years was multi-faceted Francis E. O'Connor. O'Connor, an ambitious realty brokerage dealer from San Francisco, bought large tracts of land in the area late in 1937. Then through a series of oversized bold-printed quarter-paged ads and long hours of travel throughout the north state, he convinced businessmen to invest commercially and he persuaded job seekers to buy lots in his tracts. Working from a two-room tract office, O'Connor braved the muddy mucky dirt roads to make regular trips to Redding in search of new clients.

All through 1938 and into 1939 competition flared between Summit City and Central Valley entrepreneurs for economic leadership. By mid-1939 Central Valley clearly contained the majority of gas stations, stores, restaurants and "drinking establishments" (Shasta Historical Society).

O'Connor's quarter-page ads came under criticism from Red- ding businessmen when references were made to the "future greatness" of the Shasta Dam area and the good probability of obtaining a job. In one ad, O'Connor went so far as to estimate the value of the Summit City boomtown area at over $350 million, and that opportunity still existed for profit-minded opportunists.[21]

Another one of Summit City's "founding fathers" was hard- driving industrious Caylor O'Keefe. In February of 1938, with the aid of borrowed money, O'Keefe opened the doors on one of Summit City's first, and most popular, grocery stores. O'Keefe waited only one month before expanding his income potential by building and renting out a small bungalow behind his already successful store. O'Keefe, like fellow promoter O'Connor, constantly looked for new ways to encourage growth and development in Summit City. In April of 1938, O'Keefe testified before the California Railroad Commission about the necessity of establishing freight and passenger railway service between Redding and Summit City.[22]

Some of Summit City's new businesses attracted clients from all over Shasta County. While it is true that numerous customers from outside the dam area came at first more out of curiosity than any real need, so also is it true that boomtown shops, stores, and eateries gained a faithful following. Charley's Place, owned by newcomer Charley Holden, quickly gained local notoriety with his unusual register. With his beer hall still under construction in June of 1938, his first clients picked up pieces of scrap lumber and signed their names to it. These first wooden registers were tacked up on his walls. Word spread and soon dozens of dam workers and Redding area residents visited Charley's Place, with scraps of lumber, in hopes of adding their names to the growing wooden register. Even high level P.C.I. personnel, such as Superintendent Frank Crowe, and Bureau engineers made a point of scrawling their signatures, to the delight of the owner.[23]

Summit City businessmen quickly organized and saw the benefit of coordinating interests with Redding. The local Business Men's Association invited W. J. Elliot, manager of the Redding Retailer's Credit Association, to speak at one of their regular meetings. Elliot realizing the mutual benefit of collaborating on business interests suggested that the local Summit City group join the Redding business organization, offering their assistance and services. Shortly after this meeting, the Summit City group acting upon a suggestion from Elliot formed a credit association stating that it was necessary to keep track of "dead beats" in the dam area.[24] Elliot's coaxing can be traced to Redding's previous experience dealing with the hundreds of unemployed migrants earlier in 1938. One item that the Summit City business organization acted on was to invite the local A.F.L. to relocate headquarters in Summit City. President Joe Abplanalp, and other officers of the Summit City business group realized that local A.F.L. officials were not happy about certain restrictive union ordinances and hoped to capitalize on the situation.

Serving as the entrance to the "Dam Area" from Highway 99, entrepreneurs assumed that Project City would boom more than Central Valley or Summit City. However, while the town did proper in the early years, by 1942 it was clear that Central Valley dominated the business interests of the area (Shasta Historical Society).

Simultaneous with the rapid development in and around Summit City, was the eruption of activity in Project City. Located at the intersection of Highway 99 and the new Shasta Dam Boulevard, Project City advertised itself as the "gateway to Shasta Dam." The town's strategic location, beckoned commercial development as businessmen correctly presumed the convenience and desirability of locating near Highway 99. The town strung out along both sides of Shasta Dam Boulevard for about one half mile and extended southward several blocks. Merchants quickly utilized most of the available frontage on Shasta Dam Boulevard as commercial establishments.

In addition to the usual beer halls, dance halls, grocery stores, and gas stations so typical of boomtown development, Project City boasted the first private hospital in the boomtown area. By August of 1938, Dr. Donald B. Marchus established an emergency hospital at the junction of Highway 99 (Pacific Highway) and Shasta Dam Boulevard. Dr. Marchus arrived from southern California where he had worked as Physician In-Charge at the All-American Canal. Marchus, in talking with workers on the canal project, realized that medical services would be needed at the Shasta Dam project. His facility filled an important void for residents who had not yet been hired to work on the dam, and so, could not use the contractor's hospital at Shasta Dam Village.[25]

With good building weather in the summer of 1938 commercial buildings sprang up as fast as the lumber could be obtained and building loans secured. The Giessner Brother's Lumber Company of Project City, the first large lumber company in the dam area, supplied materials for many of the commercial buildings including the oversized and highly ornate Dama Grande Inn.[26] The Dama Grande Inn, located at the corner of Shasta Dam Boulevard and Highway 99, opened for business that same summer. The Inn, extremely popular with many dam area residents—particularly single men provided, according to some former patrons, ongoing entertainment downstairs in a lavishly decorated dance hall, and "after-hours entertainment" upstairs in highly ornate rooms.

The Dama Grande Inn welcomed workers and visitors to the Shasta Dam area, as noted in the sign (Shasta Historical Society).

In an attempt to corner most of the commercial business in rapidly expanding Project City, Roy Orr purchased a large tract of commercial land near the intersection of Highway 99 and Shasta Dam Boulevard from Redding realtor and boomtown developer W. T. Lanning. Orr, a southern California businessman, decided that Project City needed a place that could offer one-stop shopping. To this end, he planned and built a huge one-story stucco building that, when completed, offered a barbershop, electrical store, confectionery, plumbing shop, restaurant, saloon, real estate office, and an insurance office.[27]

While both Project City and Summit City sprang up out of nothing and expanded quickly to house and serve dam workers, neither town could economically compete with Central Valley. Located between Project City and Summit City, and strung out for three miles on Grand Coulee Boulevard (later renamed Shasta Dam Blvd.), Central Valley dominated the dam area commercially. Known from the start as "the boomtown" developers and speculators had a field day promoting the boomtown area both locally, statewide, and nationally.

Attracting workers to saloons and "entertainment houses" proved no problem, as numerous businesses, such as the Silver Dollar Club [far left] boasted standing room only most nights of the week (Shasta Historical Society).

The boomtown area had been home to scores of squatter camps that had appeared once the government had graded the main road from Highway 99. Here, literally out of the bushes, a new town rose. Whereas, Summit City and Project City commercially never rose above a very low-order economic threshold, Central Valley provided low to high level goods and services.[28] For example, Central Valley boasted two movie theatres, both built in the boomtown heyday year of 1938, while the town was just forming. The Shasta Theatre, serving the west side of Central Valley, sat 390 patrons, was air- cooled; and to owner Les Pancake's happy surprise, it proved to be an instant success, even though it offered only "B" movies. Running movies on Wednesday evenings and all day Saturday and Sunday, Pancake's theatre helped to provide cheap and readily available entertainment, one particularly welcomed by boomtown children and exhausted mothers.[29] A second theatre opened on the east side of the Southern Pacific railroad tracks in anticipation of continued growth in the Hardenbrook residential tract. Known as the Eastside Theatre, it never gained the popularity of the Shasta Theatre, but nevertheless, it helped establish a feeling of permanent growth in the area.

The highlight of early commercial development in Boomtown crystallized with the announcement that a shopping center would be built and anchored by the national food chain store, Safeway. Known as the Shasta Center, the complex included a hotel, attached shops and offices, a double row of duplex cabins with "real luxury, showers."[30] At one end of the complex stood the Safeway store which offered a "full line of products."[31] Officials realized from the beginning that a permanent town was "in the making." They also wanted to attract business from Redding, and so, full page advertisements and flyers appeared regularly in Redding newspapers. The Shasta Center containing a number of shops including a: coffee shop, beer hall, barber, clothing store, shoe repair, beauty parlor, dress shop, and ice cream parlor, advertised throughout the year.

Boomtown entrepreneurs went to great pains to secure commercial dominance in the dam area. Aware of the fact that Project City's prime location on the corner of Highway 99 and Shasta Dam Blvd. and Summit City's buildings sitting at the other strategic spot at the corner of Shasta Dam Blvd. and the Kennett-Buckeye Road, Central Valley businessmen spent large sums of money selling their area. They pooled their money to put up signs declaring "Boomtown Center, 'The Hub of Commercial Activity' Water Service Now Available, Choice Business Locations and Ideal Homesites."[32]

This sign said it all—"The Hub of Commercial Activity" (Shasta Historical Society).

In an attempt to legitimize their pronouncements about commercial leadership in the dam area local residents led by the Central Valley business organization in November of 1938 presented to the county board of supervisors the necessary number of signatures requesting a special election to allow Central Valley to incorporate. Attorney H. M. Simon, representing the Central Valley group, argued that this would be the first step in establishing the boomtown as a "modern city." Simon added that incorporation benefits included adequate police and fire protection; it also allowed for an "organized body to act for the city in bringing money and population to the area."[33] It would also ensure commercial dominance over neighboring Summit City and Project City.[34]

The Mint Pool Hall remained a popular Friday and Saturday night entertainment center for single men, offering beer, pool and cards (Shasta Historical Society).

The Central Valley incorporation announcement created a minor uproar in nearby Redding. The thought that the rapidly expanding boomtown had sufficient population to incorporate at such an early date from its creation frightened many Redding businessmen and local residents that they were about to be overshadowed. Redding residents had assumed from the very start of the Shasta Dam project that the main benefactor, in terms of growth in the commercial sector, would be Redding. Now Central Valley appeared overnight out of nowhere and boasted a population of over 1,750 in only a few months of existence.[35] Fears increased with the sobering thought that only preliminary work had begun on the dam; what would happen when full-scale concrete work would begin in early 1939?

With the very hot summer temperatures kids and adults spent their money on homemade ice cream and ice cold Coca-Cola at the Dam Shack (Shasta Historical Society).

Long-time and well-liked county clerk E. A. Yank added to the confusion when he publicly stated that he didn't know the legal procedure for incorporation. In his fourteen-year tenure as county clerk for Shasta County he had never received an incorporation request. Looking back through the county records, Yank was able to determine that the last town to be incorporated was the copper mining boomtown of Kennett, that being in the year 1911. Checking elsewhere for more recent incorporations, he revealed that Tule Lake had gone through the process in 1937 and he contacted officials there for information.[36]

Mud became a soggy fact-of-life, especially before paved roads appeared on Shasta Dam Blvd. Residents discovered that the yearly rainfall amounts nearly doubled that of nearby Redding (Shasta Historical Society).

At the time of the incorporation request, Central Valley residents counted no less than 70 commercial enterprises, including: two lumber yards, three hotels, eight grocery stores, nineteen restaurants, five markets, seven real estate offices, five service stations, three plumbing and electrical shops, one hospital, one garage, one law firm, one post office, one hardware store, two theatres, dozens of beer halls and assorted shops.[37] This number surpassed the combined number of businesses in both Project City and Summit City. On November 17, 1938, a well attended meeting supporting incorporation took place in Central Valley. In addition to the scores of local supporters, Francis J. Carr, vice-chairman of the state Democratic Central Committee and one of the central figures in the creation of the Central Valley Water Project, attended. Also present were local A.F.L. representatives, excited over the possibility of incorporation for Central

Valley. They hoped to move their headquarters from Redding where "unfair organizing licensing ordinances" prevailed.[38]

Shortly after the New Year in 1939, Central Valley businessmen, awaiting the county decision on incorporation and adopting a tact of respectability, requested that the local newspapers refrain from calling their fair town, Boomtown. From this date forward the name Central Valley appeared in most articles referring to the area. A few days later, on January 7, 1939 the bad news was announced. The county board of supervisors rejected the incorporation bid because of "incorrect boundary descriptions," as determined by county surveyor Ernest Breuning. In their hasty enthusiasm, numerous business owners and developers had supplied crude, and usually overestimated boundary delineations on semi-official maps. Upon hearing the sad news, Central Valley incorporation proponents advised the county board that a new petition with corrected descriptions would be presented.[39] However, as time went on, business leaders and residents began to consider the additional costs that would be incurred through improved services and the incorporation debate continued until World War II.

In the middle of Central Valley's incorporation bid a tragic accident occurred depriving the community of one of its strongest supporters. State Senator John B. McColl, a local Democratic favorite in his second term, died in an automobile accident. McColl's tireless work, along with Francis Carr had convinced President Roosevelt and a reluctant Congress to build Shasta Dam as an integral part of the Central Valley Project. Governor Frank Merriam, upon hearing of McColl's untimely death, commented, "The Central Valley Project will be a perpetual monument to McColl...Senator McColl was one of the outstanding, if not the most unselfish and serious champion of the great water conservation and power project." Merriam added, "He was almost single-handedly responsible for the action of the 1938 legislature in submitting the Central Valley Project constitutional amendment to the people and for passing the necessary legislation for the undertaking."[40]

Bureau of Reclamation Commissioner John C. Page expressed shock over McColl's passing and remarked "His unselfish devotion to the best interests of the project won him many friends." Page went on to describe McColl as a "vital factor" in shaping the 170 million dollar Central Valley Project and in encouraging growth in and around the dam site.[41] McColl's funeral, held in Redding, was well attended by Central Valley residents.

Central Valley had its share of saloons, beer halls, dance halls, and cafes. As was true of typical gold mining boomtowns of the nineteenth century and oil boomtowns of the early twentieth century, early commercial buildings were simple wooden affairs sporting vertical facade fronts on which the establishment's name appeared in bold letters. At this stage in the boomtown's growth there were no sidewalks or paved streets. The Silver Dollar beer hall, one of the favorite meeting and drinking places, thrived in this environment.

By September of 1938, development revealed a more advanced stage of commercial layout. The buildings were much closer, revealing the higher value of land, covered porches and concrete entryways were now prevalent and while Shasta Dam Blvd. had not yet been paved, the road had been leveled and graveled.

Commercial evolution, or at least the sophistication of the way business is practiced, is an interesting phenomenon to watch develop within the relatively unrestricted financial environment of boomtowns. In addition to the physical evolution as noted above, one can point to instances of experimental commercial approaches, particularly during early boomtown development. These first entrepreneurs, unsure of the market needs and threshold limits of a new region, experimented with many types of businesses. This initial period in the business life of the boomtown communities revealed many new enterprises. Take for instance the Big Dipper Ice Cream Shop opened by Rudi Raki. Raki, a veteran dam builder having worked on the giant Ft. Peck earth dam and massive Grand Coulee, followed the northern migration route to Shasta County. Here, having suffered through the long hot valley summer in 1938, Raki discussed the possibility of opening up an ice cream shop with area residents. Pooling his cash resources Raki bought a lot on Shasta Dam Blvd., where he and his wife quickly realized a resounding response from the just-forming boomtown community.[42] Their success was further increased when Raki installed one of the few telephones available.[43] When Mrs. Raki entered and won top prize for ice cream flavor recipes at the 1939 state fair, the Big Dipper's future was assured. Raki's success prompted reluctant would-be business owners to take action. Not long after the opening of the Big Dipper, gambling entrepreneurs risked thousands investing in an outdoor skating rink. The Central Valley Skating Rink supplied profits to its investors for several years.

Most nineteenth century mining boomtowns of the Rocky Mountain region revealed an initial single street business development, the so-called "main street" phenomena. Strung out along both sides of dusty Shasta Dam Blvd. Central Valley's saloons, grocery stores, meat markets, boardinghouses, and restaurants look surprisingly similar to the same kinds of businesses shown in photographs of Virginia City, Montana in the late 1860s and Alta, Utah in 1873.[44] Along the main street single-owned small stores and shops opened first, typically bars, saloons, dance halls, general stores, etc. Such was true in all of the dam area boomtowns, particularly Central Valley. Jake Polin's Little Reno, Clyde Akin's Bar, The Dam

Shack, The Shadows (dance hall), the Silver Dollar (beer hall) and the always crowded and often rowdy Mint Pool Hall formed the nucleus of the new community.

The long, sweeping driveway in front of the popular Shasta Dam Market invited local drivers to pull-in and pickup last minute food and dry-goods before heading home (Shasta Historical Society).

As 1939 began Central Valley's business district showed signs of advanced commercial development. As in the case with Summit City and Project City, word of business opportunities spread throughout the northstate, partnerships were formed and larger more sophisticated enterprises appeared. Frank Jones and Ben Harrison constructed one large building and located a cafe, barber shop, and recreation hall within its walls.[45] From out of the area, came Lee Griner and Del Stewart. They saw firsthand the tremendous building boom in late 1938 and promptly decided to erect a builders' supply house. Carrying a large inventory and providing honest polite service their Shasta Builders and Supply provided an example of how a successful boomtown business should function.[46]

Redding business owners with established reputations also jumped into the commercial fray in Central Valley. Probably the biggest company to attempt a branch store in the area was Redding's well-known Public Market, offering both groceries and dry-goods. Utilizing a huge half-page ad in the Redding Record newspaper, the owner of the Public Market (Jake Burkiand) proudly announced the grand opening of a second store in Central Valley. Advertising a large inventory and very low prices, the ad

75

declared that "returned products will be refunded promptly." Expecting stiff competition from the newly running Safeway, Burkland reassured boomtown residents that their market would be "modern in every way, and one of the largest in Shasta County."[47]

On the individual side, men like C. H. Campbell, a real estate salesman under J. C. Tibbitts (one of the original land developers), sensed greater opportunity by breaking out on his own. Campbell, by the end of 1938, had taken and passed his brokers license, and announced plans to open his own real estate office.[48] And, while the Public Market competed with the local Safeway for dam area grocery shoppers, one of the Market's employees decided that Central Valley needed another small singly-owned market. Mike's Market was the result. Residents remembered and appreciated his personal one-on-one service.[49]

By mid- 1939, members of the Central Valley Commercial Club could look back to August of 1938, when the business organization first formed, and recall, in astonishment, how far and how fast business development had come. The future looked bright, yet few business owners knew how long the prosperity would last.

This photo, taken in September of 1938, reveals two of the storefront facades so popular in the early boomtown development. Wimpy's restaurant served over-sized hamburgers that quickly garnered the admiration, and business of local families. The Smoke Shop, right next door continued to sell tobacco for pipes and cigarettes—you rolled you own most of the time (Bureau of Reclamation).

Store construction usually consisted of long, rectangular buildings set back only a short distance from the road. Façade front panels extended up to the roof crest, allowing the owner to advertise the business name (Bureau of Reclamation).

Chapter 6
Residential Development

Even before job seekers encroached into the dam area in 1937, William Hammans, ex-City Marshal of Redding, dreamed of building a community off Highway 99 not far from where the government purchased some land in 1931. Hammans and his son Gene, decided in 1935 to build and run a service station with a lunch-counter and a small grocery store. He called the fledgling hamlet, Midway.[1] From his meadow location, Hammans made ends meet supplying the needs of travelers heading north from Redding on Highway 99 and residents of Mountain Gate (a small community located 12 miles north of Redding). Midway remained diminutive and unimportant until the Spring of 1937 when Gene Hammans learned of the government's decision to cut, grade, and gravel a major road through part of his property adjacent to Highway 99. The young Hammans realized the significance of the government decision and moved quickly to secure the services of W. T. Lanning, successful real estate broker.

With the dual purpose of satisfying his father's wishes of creating a community and the very real possibility of turning a quick profit, Hammans and Lanning planned the first major subdivision. As hundreds of incoming job hopefuls swarmed near his property setting up makeshift living quarters, Hammans and Lanning announced that the "only approved subdivision in the dam district" was now open and available.[2] Known as the "Hammans Tract" it fronted on what would be Grand Coulee Blvd. and proved to be quite popular. Lot sales began at the end of July in 1937, increased in intensity during August and September, and by November, only a few lots remained.

PROJECT CITY SELECTED AS NAME OF AREA-- "HAMMANS" LOSES BY FOUR VOTES AT MEETING WEDNESDAY

Property owners of the area adjacent to the intersection of Highway 99 and the Kennett road, nine miles north of Redding, voted 56 to 52 Wednesday night to call the region "Project City" instead of "Hammans" the other name presented. There is an estimated population of 1500 persons

Over 200 attended the meeting, but only property owners were allowed to vote on the naming of the community. The new district embraces the towns formerly called Project City, north and west of the intersection and Highway City east of Highway 99.

The community includes land a quarter mile north of the Kennett road; a quarter mile to the west; a half mile south, to the start of Grand Coulee boulevard and a quarter mile east of Highway 99.

Wednesday night's meeting was an open air gathering, held back of the real estate office at the intersection of the two main highways.

Dr. Donald Marchus presided and W.K. Gaslan assisted him in arrangements for the meeting.

It was announced at the meeting that a postoffice has been approved for the community, necessitating the agreement on a name to cover all the various subdivisions.

A committee was appointed to post roads in the area with safety signs

-- The Courier-Free Press, Thursday, April 13, 1939

78

The process of spatial community growth can be analyzed effectively by mapping the chronological development of approved subdivisions. The boomtown subdivisions map for 1937 depicts the Shasta Dam area through the summer and fall of that year, at the very beginning of community genesis. Hamman's original subdivision can be seen lining Highway 99 and affronting up to the proposed road site of Grand Coulee Blvd. Calculating rapid growth in the area, Hamman's surmised that the junction of Highway 99 and Grand Coulee Blvd. would naturally serve as the core of a new boomtown. He moved to develop adjacent acreage, Hamman's Subdivision #2. Meanwhile, William L. Hill, already involved in pursuing commercial interests in the booming Summit City area, organized the first subdivision in that area later in August of 1937.

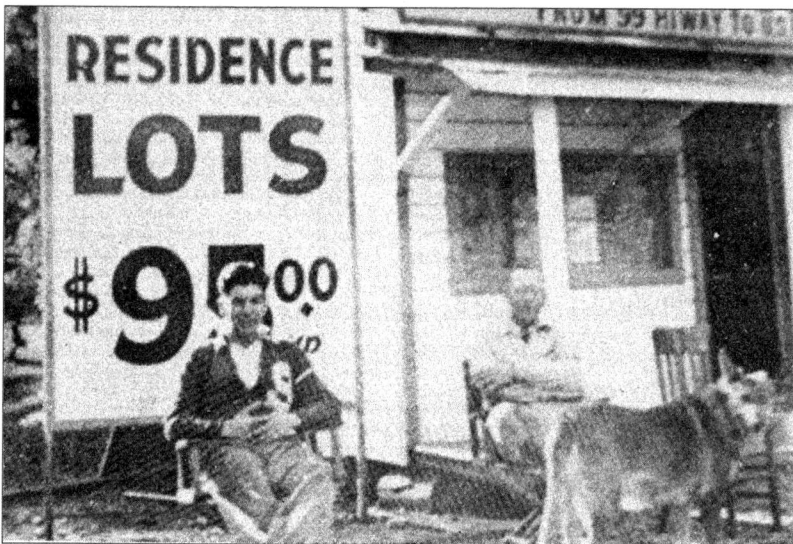

Five dollars down, along with $5.00 a month became the standard financial commitment for dam workers desiring to buy a "tree covered lot." Leland Kronschnable (right), land speculator, with dog Fang and friend, Vic Miller (Les Pancake/Hazel McKim).

A group of local Redding investors led by J. V. Stanton purchased frontage on Grand Coulee Blvd. near the Hamman's tract, planned a large subdivision, and called it Boomtown. Actually, the Hamman and Stanton tracts would evolve into Project City. The town Boomtown, or Central Valley, formed about a mile west of Project City. But, at the time, many investors referred to their tracts as boomtowns, as the pace of home-building quickened.

With the word out about the government grading of Grand Coulee Blvd. and the widening of the Kennett Road speculators hurried to buy up large portions of land and present subdivision maps. Stanton and Hill led the way as they together pooled their resources to open two new subdivisions, Boomtown #2 and #3 in January of 1938. Along with resident Charles McConnell, the duo located their properties in juxtaposition west of the original tracts. It is here where the core of the town Central Valley would lie. The boomtown subdivisions map for January and February of 1938 clearly shows that speculation focused on frontages on Highway 99, Grand Coulee Blvd., and Kennett Road. Hill continued to develop the

Summit City area expanding with Summit #2 subdivision, while G. E. Oaks bought land on the east side of Highway 99, adding houses in what would later become Project City. Farther south, Charles Akard, gambled considerable money in developing the area he named Pine Grove.

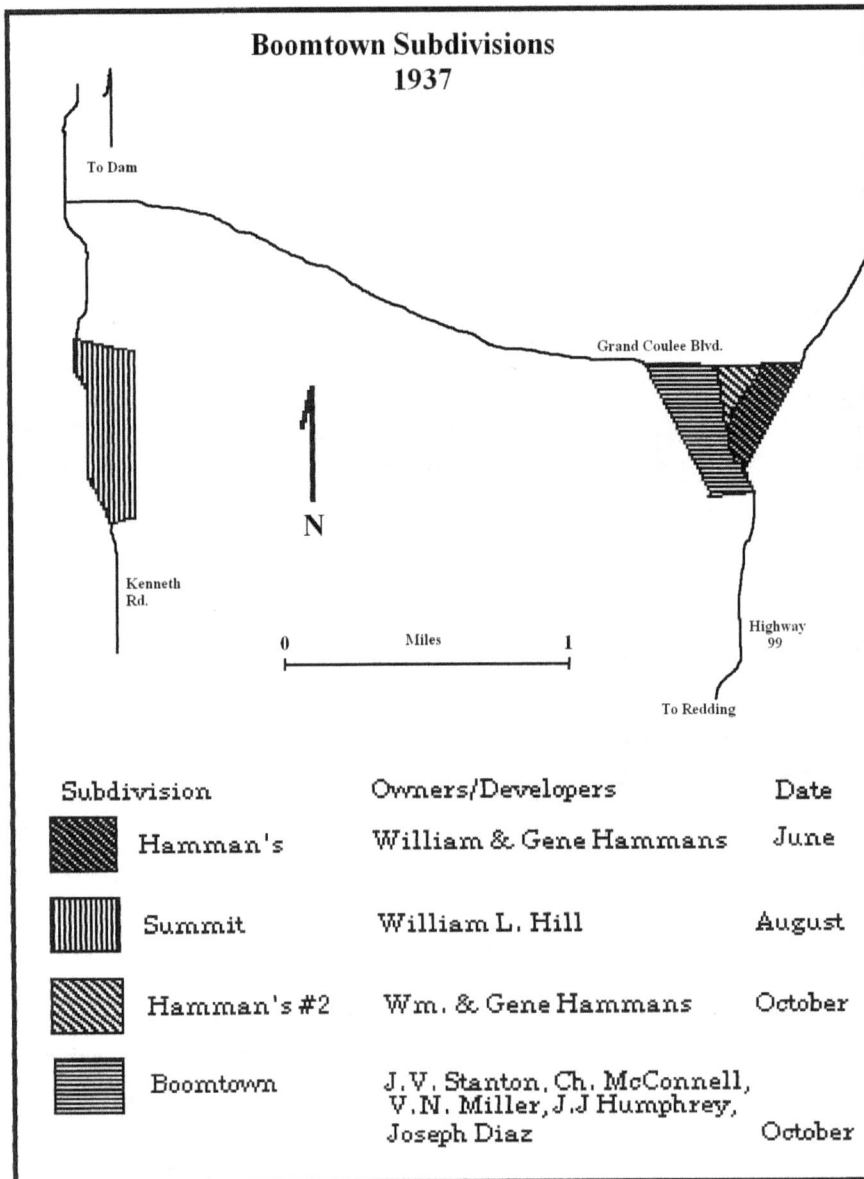

Boomtown Subdivisions
1937

To Dam

Grand Coulee Blvd.

N

Kenneth Rd.

0   Miles   1

Highway 99

To Redding

Subdivision	Owners/Developers	Date
Hamman's	William & Gene Hammans	June
Summit	William L. Hill	August
Hamman's #2	Wm. & Gene Hammans	October
Boomtown	J.V. Stanton, Ch. McConnell, V.N. Miller, J.J Humphrey, Joseph Diaz	October

Not shown on the map is the new Buckeye Subdivision located on Kennett Road about five miles south of Summit City. A community here at Buckeye would form, but commercial investment amounted to little. Also not appearing on the map is the Lakeview Subdivision, developed by Charles Diestelhorst. He realized at an early date that Redding itself would grow tremendously, and that much of that growth would naturally flow in the direction of the dam activity, north.[3]

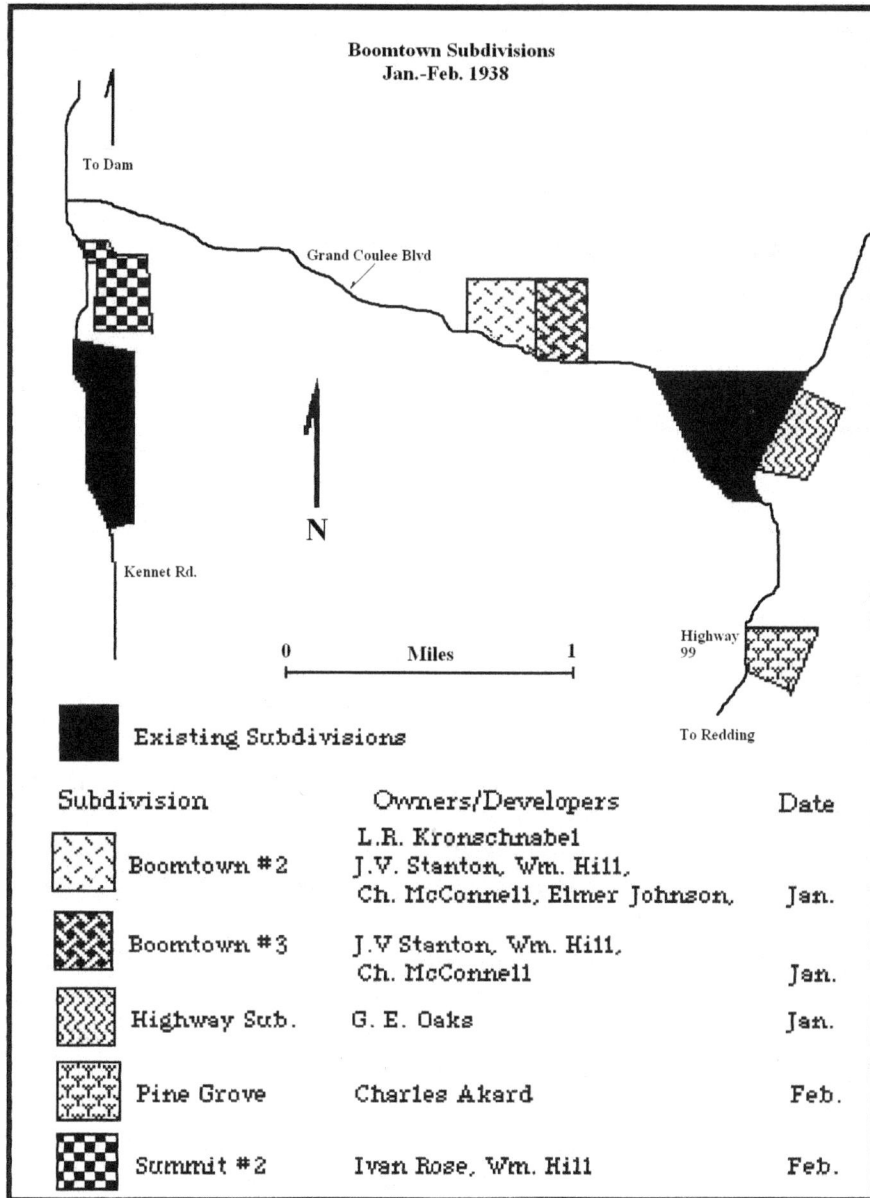

Boomtown Subdivisions
Jan.-Feb. 1938

Subdivision	Owners/Developers	Date
Boomtown #2	L.R. Kronschnabel J.V. Stanton, Wm. Hill, Ch. McConnell, Elmer Johnson.	Jan.
Boomtown #3	J.V Stanton, Wm. Hill, Ch. McConnell	Jan.
Highway Sub.	G. E. Oaks	Jan.
Pine Grove	Charles Akard	Feb.
Summit #2	Ivan Rose, Wm. Hill	Feb.

As the cold weather of winter in 1938 subsided, four new subdivisions were in the planning. Growth continued to follow the linear string pattern established in 1937. Housing activity centered now along Grand Coulee Blvd. as the Boomtown (Central Valley) tract expanded west. As seen in all the earlier tracts, lateral development extended no more than one or two streets in either direction of the main thoroughfares. Dominating

81

the area was L. R. Kronschnable, J. J. Humphreys, and Albert Rouge's Boomtown Tract #5, twice the size of any previous subdivision and located strategically along both sides of Grand Coulee Blvd. Along with numerous successful businesses that would be established on their frontage property, this tract attracted scores of settlers because of its proximity to the Government Camp (Toyon).

Hill continued to develop and dominate growth in the Summit City area. His tract Summit #3 became the first that did not front along a major transportation route. Instead, the tract linked his previous housing zones together. At the same time, April of 1938, Roy Orr moved ahead with plans to develop the north side of Grand Coulee Blvd. at its intersection with Highway 99. Realizing that the tremendous growth west of his property was evolving into a separate town, where most of the new residents were referring to the area as Boomtown, Orr opted to call his tract Project City, in reference to the dam project. His term caught on and by 1939 as work on Shasta Dam moved into high gear, residents in and around Orr's property renamed their settlement in honor of the dam project.

Newspaper advertisements began to appear in two local Red- ding newspapers offering dam area lots at reasonable rates. Francis E. O'Connor placed an ad for Summit City residential lots offering "restricted and unrestricted" sections.[4] Prices started at $150 for most lots, with a $5 down payment and payments of only $5 a month. O'Connor utilized large, easy-to-read ads, and ran them regularly from March of 1938 onward. Large numbers of job hopefuls, who were living in isolated squatter camps, now "came out of the bush", purchased lots, and began building very modest homes. Small and rectangular, many of the homes were built slowly over a time period extending many months. Would-be builders, added on as funds and/or materials became available. Many families continued to live in trailers, tents, or their cars as they erected their homes.

By the end of March, dam area residents were treated to much attention in the Redding newspapers. Headlines proclaimed "Communities in Area of Dam Thriving." The paper correctly analyzed the demographics of the dam area by stating "nearly all residents are from other states, many having previous experience at Grand Coulee, Parker, and other dams."[5] The article pointed to the poor road conditions, which were due, at least in part, to the haste in which the buildings, residential and commercial, were erected.

The article also applauded local boomtown residents who, though most were not yet employed at the dam, were nevertheless, not on relief. Only two families at that time were drawing county relief.[6] To explain the lack of families on relief and their ability to continue to survive, the article explained that most families came to Shasta County with "sufficient funds to tide them over the past winter," although many of these families practiced tight spending policies.[7]

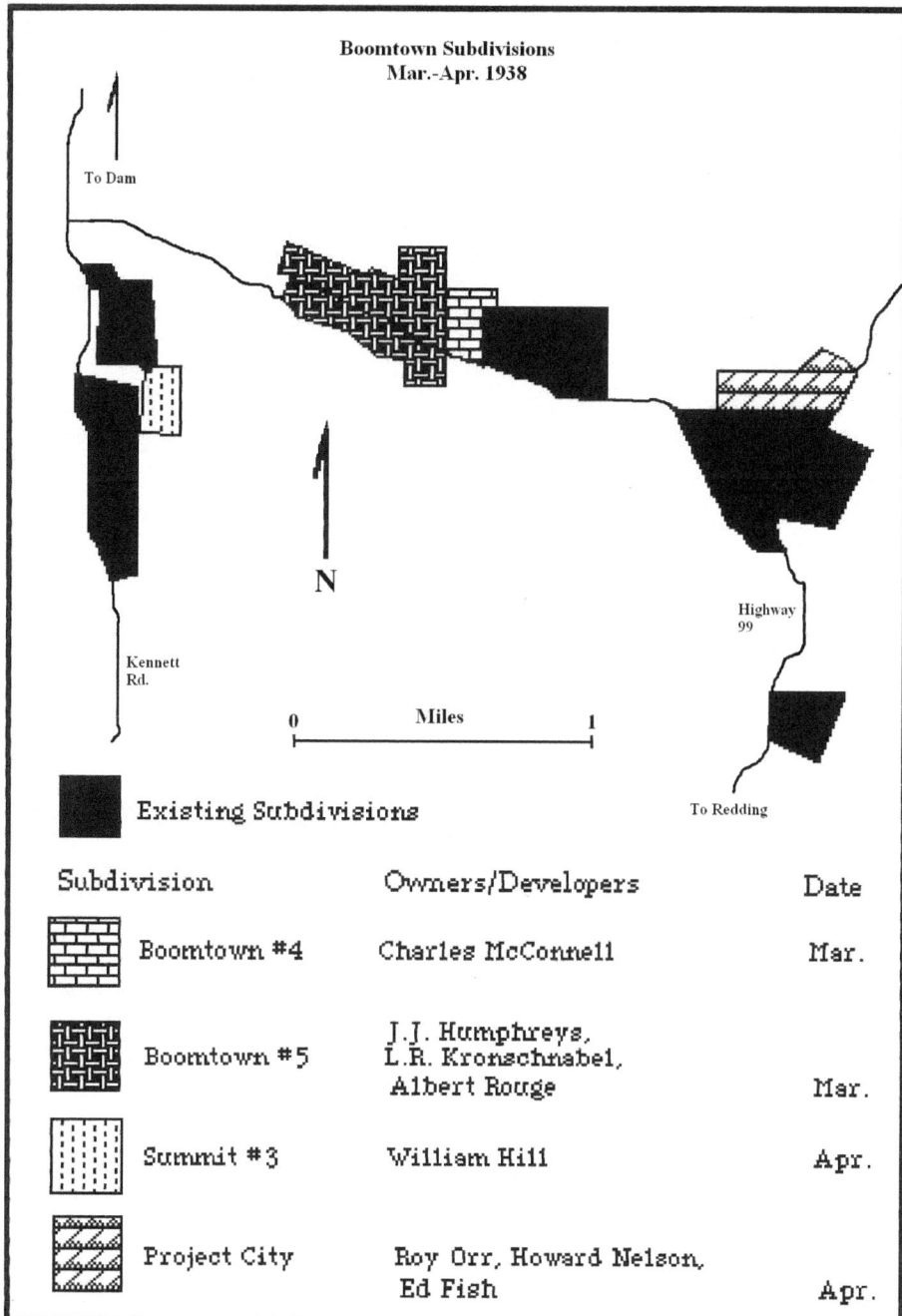

Boomtown Subdivisions
Mar.-Apr. 1938

Subdivision	Owners/Developers	Date
Boomtown #4	Charles McConnell	Mar.
Boomtown #5	J.J. Humphreys, L.R. Kronschnabel, Albert Rouge	Mar.
Summit #3	William Hill	Apr.
Project City	Roy Orr, Howard Nelson, Ed Fish	Apr.

One month later, the Searchlight interviewed Francis E. O'Connor, Summit City developer and real estate agent. Explaining that Summit City's 145 foot wide boulevard was designed to handle the expected flood of residents and shoppers, O'Connor promoted his boomtown by stating that FHA home loans were now available showcasing low interest rates and complete financing service.[8] On May 8, 1938 the Searchlight talked to W. T. Lanning Project City developer, who boasted that his lot sizes would all be located on 50 to 60 foot wide streets. He added that he planned to build a large lumber yard to handle the expected demand for building lumber.[9]

With the advent of drier weather and increased expectations for hiring on Shasta Dam residential building activity exploded. In May, the Bureau of Reclamation announced that Ralph Lowry, government engineering director at Boulder Dam, would be transferred to the Shasta project. It was commonly known that full-scale construction would not begin until Lowry arrived, so the news spread quickly through the dam area that hundreds, maybe thousands of hirings would soon take place. Interestingly enough, Lowry, like his PCI counterpart Frank Crowe, did not live in any of the boomtowns, preferring instead to live in Redding. Crowe did not live in Shasta Dam Village and Lowry did not reside in Toyon. Tremendous growth occurred during the summer of 1938. Here for the first time, new subdivisions expanded north and south of Grand Coulee Blvd. as many as five and six streets. Boomtown Subdivisions #7 and #8 linked the Boomtown with Project City providing a continuous line of residential and commercial development along Grand Coulee Blvd. Any future growth would occur in areas away from the main boulevard, and in essence, all the boomtown cores had been developed.

Growth spread so quickly that providing services to the new boomtowns proved difficult. The U. S. Post Office hurriedly opened a branch office in Boomtown (Central Valley) in July of 1938 posting 540 boxes, more to be added soon, and P.G. & E. rushed to supply power lines outward from Grand Coulee Blvd. and already occupied Toyon, which had been previously wired months before. Building construction went up so quickly that proper inspection services could not be delivered, and numerous homes encountered wiring and plumbing problems. One auto court, the Hendrickson's in Central Valley, caught fire causing considerable damage. The problem was traced to improperly installed wiring.[10]

Lot prices, as low as $35, averaged $50 to $75. Interested parties could acquire a loan by putting down $5 and making $5 payments a month. By September of 1938, speculation drove up lot prices to $95, particularly in Central Valley.[11] Lot prices included water and sewer privileges. This however, meant little as a successful water system could not be obtained from underground water pools, due to the solid rock strata located below most of the dam area As far as septic tanks go, Rumboltz reported that "water flush toilets were a rarity in the whole area.[12] Even Toyon School resorted to "outside toilets" until 1940.

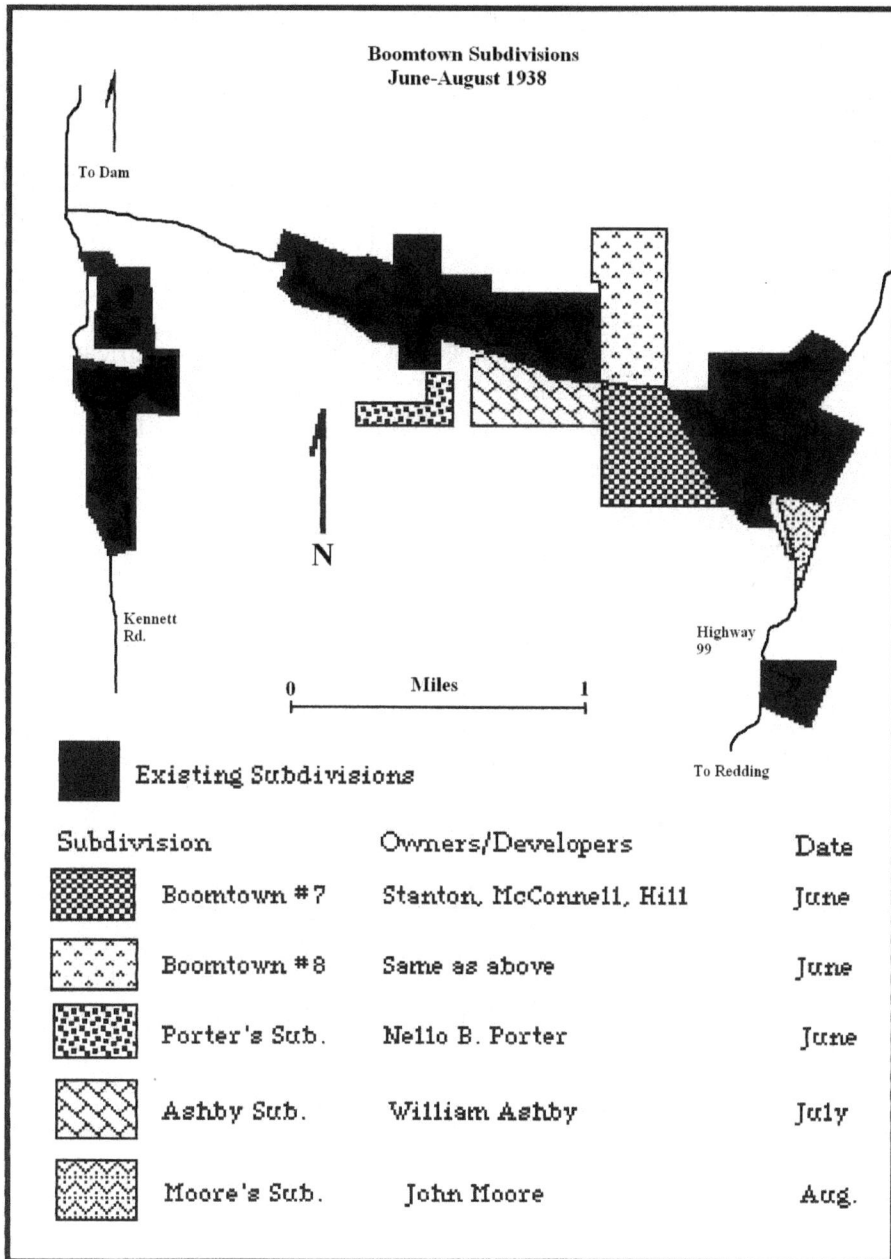

Boomtown Subdivisions
June-August 1938

To Dam

Kennett
Rd.

N

0   Miles   1

Highway
99

To Redding

■   Existing Subdivisions

Subdivision		Owners/Developers	Date
▦	Boomtown #7	Stanton, McConnell, Hill	June
⠿	Boomtown #8	Same as above	June
⠿	Porter's Sub.	Nello B. Porter	June
⧄	Ashby Sub.	William Ashby	July
⠿	Moore's Sub.	John Moore	Aug.

By November of 1938 houses in and around the boomtowns sold quickly as more and more newspaper ads competed for buyers. Many of the ads exaggerated the dam area development, such as the November 19 ad placed by developer Joe Sauer. Sauer claimed that his subdivision was the "fastest growing in all of northern California" and that the Southern Pacific Railroad route would locate a stop at his location. On both of these accounts, he was wrong. Other ads appeared stating that massive new hirings for dam work would continue and that all residents could be guaranteed a job and a new home. By December, these highly questionable ads came under sharp attack when a grand jury decision asked for a full investigation of land sales "near Shasta Dam." Preliminary investigation revealed numerous complaints that ads had misrepresented living conditions and current job possibilities. The grand jury reported that they found the ads to be "vicious and to the detriment of taxpayers of Shasta County for the reason that they attract an indigent class here who may eventually be charges on the county."[13]

At about the same time, that the grand jury was investigating speculative newspaper advertisements, news spread of a significant gold discovery on the residential property of newly arrived job seeker H. 0. Henderson. Henderson purchased one of the Central Valley lots and while installing his septic tank he unearthed "extensive quantities" of low-grade gold ore.[14] News of the gold find brought scores of visitors to Henderson's property, and neighbors busied themselves digging up their backyards in hopes of cashing-in. Further investigation discovered that Henderson's find was actually part of a large vein running diagonally through eight adjacent lots. Now speculation soared as a mining camp fever swept over the boomtown area. Rumors and stories fed much of the idle conversation for the next two months as job hopefuls dreamed of striking it rich. Nearby streams, tributaries of the Sacramento River became crowded as gold panning and stream dredging increased. Not much gold was actually recovered as the Henderson vein played out quickly and soon the reality of finding a job sobered gold-hungry boomtowners.

Also attracting the attention of many people in the winter of 1938 was the news that a comprehensive bus service would link the residential areas directly to Redding. A new partnership was formed combining the assets of Leslie Aliward, H. V. Tatcher, and E. H. Lowden. Calling their new bus company the Shasta Dam Transit Company, they promised a regular bus schedule and reliable service.[15] With the stock of boomtown stores extremely limited, many people welcomed a bus service that could provide transportation to Redding where "hard to get" supplies could be found.

In the middle of all the boomtown development, few people realized the expansion, taking place at both Shasta Dam Village (contractor's camp) and at Toyon (government camp). PCI erected another giant two-story dormitory to house another 100 single men. Over at Toyon new duplexes and single family houses were going up to house the many newly arrived transferred government engineers and inspectors. By Christmas of 1938, activity was slowing down due to the rainy weather yet, enthusiasm ran high. Everyone felt sure that the next year, 1939, would be the year of the beginning of large-scale hiring and prosperous times, which for many, had been a luxury of the distant past. One happy couple, Mr. & Mrs. Olen Ware, confident of his continued dam work (he had been hired in mid-1938), splurged and purchased a new automobile as their Christmas present to themselves.[16]

Most homes were simple rectangular two-bedroom cottages (Shasta Historical Society).

Boomtown residents with jobs rejoiced during the Christmas season over their situations and made plans that are more permanent. Dale Bryant, a veteran of both Boulder and Parker Dams, decided not to live in the contractor's camp as he had previously done. Believing that Shasta Dam would be his last dam project and longing for a permanent home site, Bryant purchased, in August of 1938, one of the first lots in Project City.[17] By now, he had a child, and with another on the way, he took out a loan to build a small cottage home. As 1938 ended for Bryant, he felt sure that life would now finally settle down. Anderson Pike, like many Depression job seekers, left his family behind when traveling to the Shasta Dam site in 1938. Once securing a job, Pike invested in a lot in Central Valley and began building a comfortable three-bedroom home. Pike then sent for his family who joined him in time for the holidays.[18]

No one seemed more pleased at the way the dam area was developing, and had more to be thankful for than J. C. Tibbitts. As one of the first real estate brokers and promoters of the dam area, he took great pleasure in helping people realize the dream of purchasing their own boomtown home. Tibbitts' real estate office with the large letters "BOOMTOWN" spelled out on top was a landmark for many months. At one time or another, he was involved in property management and home insurance. Tibbitts' warm personality and honest dealings endeared him to many newcomers confused by all the hoopla and misrepresentations prevalent throughout 1938 and 1939. He was later voted in to serve as local justice court judge for the boomtown area, and by the end of 1938 he could look back and see that three substantial new towns had been laid out and were now prospering, as a result of his tireless work.[19] Tibbitts later solved the chronic water problem in the boomtown area in 1950, by arranging for a government contract to bring water into the boomtowns from newly rising Shasta Lake.

Boomtown homes in or near Central Valley, 1938-1940 (Bureau of Reclamation).

Small hillside homes with a sweeping view remained popular with boomtown families. Many of the lots ranged from one to several acres (Bureau of Reclamation).

Chapter 7
Life in the Boomtowns
Schools and Churches

The majority of Shasta Dam workers were white blue-collar workers many of whom had previous dam experience. Almost everyone residing in the boomtowns worked on the dam itself or provided services and goods to those who did work on the dam. Hundreds of workers knew each other from other dam jobs, and all lived at about the same socio-economic level.[20]

Several groups of ethnic minorities did work on the dam, yet their numbers remained small and little is known of their social environment. The main reason for a lack of information on the few minority group dam workers arises from the fact that little socializing occurred between the white workers and their minority counterparts. Few, if any, non-whites remained in the area after the dam was completed and none were available for interviews. Scores of Mexicans, mostly hired after a perceived labor shortage during World War II, did find employment. These workers came from areas as far south as Los Angeles.[21] Black participation on the building of Shasta Dam proved to amount to less than a dozen. The blacks, like their Mexican counterparts, remained "out of sight" except during working hours, and little is known about their residences or social habits. There appears to have been no reported racial incidents involving confrontations or violence.[22]

The largest contingent of ethnic non-white minorities to work on the dam and live in the boomtown area were the Wintu Indians. Employment records are no longer available, yet it is apparent that dozens of Indians worked on Shasta Dam and lived, for the most part, in and around Summit City. Some Indians that secured employment had Anglicized names such as Sisk, Montgomery, and Popejoy. They rounded-up scrap lumber, much as had the earlier white squatters, and built simple, yet livable homes. White neighbors remembered an interesting custom. When a family member would die, the house would be abandoned and burned. This tradition, long practiced by northern California Indians, came under sharp criticism by government officials nervous about uncontrolled fires near a government project.[23] Indian workers and residents adjusted well on the Shasta Dam job, and no troubles were reported. However, when it was learned that several sacred burial grounds would be covered by the soon-to-be rising waters of

Shasta Lake, Indians demanded government action. Shasta Bureau engineer Ralph Lowry promptly responded by transferring the Indian remains to a safe site in Central Valley (west end of Boca Street).[24]

Typical dam workers were white males, usually between the ages of 18 and 35. Ray Rogers considered himself to be representative of the dam workers. He recalled that most were young, restless, and eager to acquire "another dam job." He had previous dam experience on the Imperial Dam, a diversionary dam for the All-American Canal. Rogers possessed honed skills, including plumbing and mechanical experience.[25]

The Hoover, Parker, and now Shasta workers who followed veteran dam builder Frank Crowe retained a sense of group identity. Having lived and worked together for years, they considered themselves "one big happy

91

family."[26] Veteran dam workers dressed alike, utilized the same skills and often socialized. Men who were able to secure a position would write home to bring out their families. This was the case with Harold W. Fortier, who was able to secure a job for his brother.[27] More often than not, their immediate family was accompanied to Shasta County by extended family members; all hoping for work. All of the boomtowns showed evidence of extended family settlement. The hiring staff became quite acquainted with the above fact, as numerous workers would come into the 'hiring shack' and seek employment for a relative or friend. One job seeker, L. T. Thornton, using a friend's identification work badge, was able to acquire his first dam job (at Grand Coulee) by pretending to be an established worker and convincing the hiring manager that he knew of a skilled and talented mechanic's friend desperately in need of work. When the supervisor told him to send his friend in to see him sometime, Thornton looked at him and replied, "I am that friend." He was hired immediately.[28]

Many Shasta Dam men and women formed life-long friendships resulting from years of close working relationships. In this photograph, two workers enjoy a short coffee break from unloading incoming materials (Bureau of Reclamation).

One of the earliest forms of civic and democratic participation in the boomtown area was the Summit City Businessmen Association. This group led by Joe Abplanalp conducted regular meetings from early 1938 on. Topics for discussion and action included much more than the promotion of their personal interests. From the start, they talked about improving roads, acquiring a reliable water supply, preventing crime, and planning for future community growth.[29] Local Summit City residents looked to these businessmen to solve reoccurring problems and to provide a liaison with county officials. William Hill, responsible for developing most of the land in Summit City residential lots, worked effectively with the local business association organizing community groups to deal with pressing concerns. Hill's discussions with county officials helped to bring about the widening and improving of Kennett Road, an important transportation link with Redding. Hill also urged local businessmen to secure county help in obtaining streetlights for the business section of Summit City. In an attempt to encourage community spirit and involvement, the business association sponsored several social events, of which the annual Christmas party was the most successful.[30]

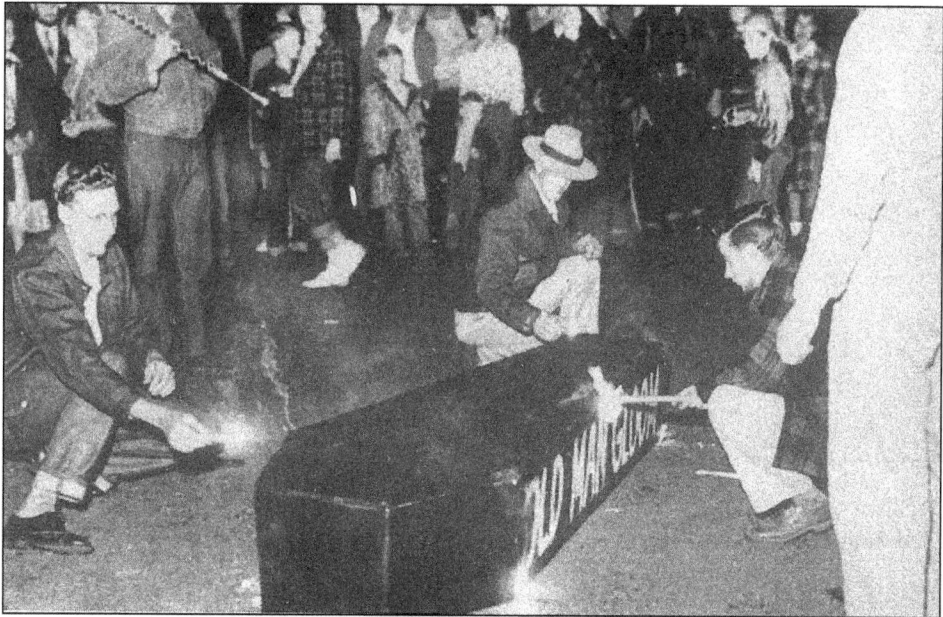

The 1938 "Burning Old Man Gloom" celebration symbolized boomtown residents' desire to dismiss the economic doldrums of the Great Depression and look to the future of jobs and security (Hazel McKim).

At Project City, Dr. Donald B. Marchus, realizing the need for a quality medical facility, built and ran the boomtown's first and only hospital. Here residents not employed on the dam and thus not qualified for medical care at the contractor's hospital, received competent medical care for reasonable rates. Marchus, and Ray Orr, a newly arrived businessman from southern California, worked to build a Project City Businessmen's Association that communicated regularly with their respective counterparts in Summit City and Central Valley. Together these business groups, oftentimes, merged to form political affiliations. The Shasta Dam Democratic Club, led for the most part by successful business owners in the boomtown area, held mass meetings to discuss school support and highway improvements.[31]

Jonathan Tibbitts (left), a boomtown community leader, often organized and led local events, such as the "Hell's Gulch Celebration shown above (Hazel McKim).

In Central Valley, a real estate broker rose to provide leadership during the boomtown's formative years. Jonathan Tibbitts had become involved at Central Valley early in 1937 as a land speculator and real estate agent. He knew that lots and homes sales would remain brisk as long as the government was hiring. Tibbitts also revealed genuine interest in becoming involved in the community's affairs, and planning for its future. From an early date, Tibbitts realized that one of the major problems would be the acquiring a reliable water source. He initiated talks with federal dam representatives and continued the dialogue until, as will be shown later, he secured an agreement that guaranteed sufficient water supplies. Tibbitts' efforts were rewarded in 1938 when he was voted-in as Justice-Of-The-Peace for the area. By this time, he had won the respect and confidence of his neighbors.[32] Tibbitts stated that community leadership was both an honor and a shared experience. He stated that the majority of residents showed an active interest in participating and oftentimes shared leadership responsibilities. Tibbitts pointed to Wynn Price and others who worked with county, state, and federal officials to improve life in the boomtowns, everything from increasing mail deliveries to organizing a complete water district plan.[33]

The "Hell's Gulch" celebration (the name refers to the high summer temperatures and the valley-like topography) prompted boomtown residents to put their money back into banks (Hazel McKim).

Tibbitts indicated that as in the case of "traditional democracy," political leadership did not depend on a certain level of wealth or recognized status. Blue-collar dam workers (non-supervising personnel) met with white-collar boomtown business owners to discuss and act on pressing community problems. Oftentimes the meetings were quite informal, over beer and music, at a local beer hail or tavern. It is also interesting to note that even though most of the dam workers fully expected to be moving on to another dam job shortly, they still involved themselves

95

in the running of the community. This trend can be traced back to earlier jobs where these hardworking men learned that only through a concerted, united effort can their living conditions be made tolerable.

On of the first business that excited boomtown residents—men, women and children, was the opening of the Shasta Theater (Les Pancake).

One of the first signs of large-scale public support and involvement in the Shasta Dam area centered on providing a proper educational facility for the hundreds of dam workers' children. From the beginning Toyon School, the first to be built in the area, provided an example of large-scale public support and involvement. In 1937, there were no schools in the immediate area; the nearest one-room school houses were at Bass and Buckeye (several miles away). Working in concert in the best democratic tradition Bureau officials, PCI contracting supervisors, boomtown business leaders, and scores of concerned Shasta Dam area residents held several mass meetings and concluded plans for construction of a four-room schoolhouse. Everyone seemed to contribute to the successful completion of Toyon School. The federal government donated the land; the school would be located a short distance from the government camp and Summit City. The Bureau also supplied most of the building materials while PCI workers poured the foundation and erected the rough framing. Local businessmen, numerous off-duty workers, and others not yet employed on the dam, gave generously of their time in order to complete the task in time for students to start the 1938 academic year.

Matt Rumboltz, Toyon's first principal, and three teachers planned to open the school on October 3 of 1938. Advanced signups totaled 125 prospective students. When the school doors opened on October 10, students stormed the not-yet-finished schoolhouse.[34] Eleven days later the student population climbed to 213 and by the end of the month, 256 students had enrolled.[35] With the word out that a new school had opened, the student population steadily climbed to over 350 by the end of the year, and peaked to 400 in January of 1939, making it one of the largest rural schools in the nation.[36] By this time, the Toyon school board reacted by expanding its teaching staff to ten full-time employees, and constructing two new rooms as students were literally, "coming out of the windows." Individual classroom sizes ranged from a low of 36 to an unbelievable 73 students in one first grade class![37] Even Rumboltz's hurriedly converted his office into classroom space. The principal had to conduct his business in the hallway or outside under a tree.

Matt Rumboltz continued for many years as principal of Toyon School. Here he shown with his staff of teacher in April of 1941 (Shasta Historical Society).

Bureau officials offered Rumboltz the opportunity of moving the oversized first grade class temporarily to the community hall at Government Camp. Meanwhile enrollments continued to rise as 1939 began. At one point, Rumboltz was simply overwhelmed. He carried all the official responsibilities of principal while he also taught the eighth grade class of sixty-seven students. Fourteen of the students sat at two carefully designed tables in what used to be his office; he stood at the doorway and directed the class from both directions![38]

Realizing the intense pressure Rumboltz and the other teachers were under the boomtown communities responded with labor, donations, and assistance in the classroom. With no water facilities at all, older students had been forced to carry water in from a nearby farmhouse well. Again, a united effort saved the situation. PCI workers dug a well, the Bureau donated pipes and a pump, while residents helped install the system. Later, through community action, drinking fountains and bathrooms would also be added.

Matt Rumboltz, principal and Teacher, is shown here with the 1938 class of 7th and 8th grade students (Shasta Historical Society).

On the first back-to-school night, a huge parent turnout materialized showing enormous public support and involvement. This support would soon crystallize into a very successful Parent Teachers Association (PTA). Support was indeed widespread as parents from the government camp and from the contractor's camp mixed with boomtown residents.[39] A community spirit had been initiated. This community cooperation and involvement was not unique to the Shasta Dam boomtown experience. Mrs. Macie Montgomery, Shasta County Schools Superintendent in 1938, received a letter from the Grand Coulee Public Schools Office recounting the difficult problem they had in dealing with their huge influx of dam workers' children. Student populations there exploded to over 1000 students. The contractor there, Six Companies, assumed much of the burden of the cost, hiring and paying teachers "in reality it is a private school."[40] At Grand Coulee the Bureau had built a separate school for their workers, while the contractors' children and those from the boomtowns attended the other school. Shasta Dam residents could take special pride. They had worked with the Bureau to build a school that would be attended by children from all the boomtowns, the contractor's camp, and the government camp.

To help relieve the massive overcrowding at Toyon School, another united community effort organized. Concerned citizens drew up plans to build another elementary school farther east in Central Valley. Local Shasta Mine and Smelter's Union donated labor and some materials, while unemployed union members worked full speed to complete the job.[41] The school, Central Valley Elementary, consisted of a 24 x 80 structure with folding partitions, making it adaptable for community use.

Boomtown children, shown here participating in a art activity at the Toyon Day Care Center, endured many hardships and shortages, particularly during the formative years of 1938-1940 (Bureau of Reclamation).

Toyon's first meeting of the PTA brought out over 300 persons in attendance. In an effort to show an inter-city cooperation, the elected officers for the organization were nominated and elected from Toyon, Central Valley, and Summit City.[42] In January of 1939, the PTA raised money to help provide and install toilets for the new school. By the end of the school year the organization helped by stocking needed supplies, aiding in the classrooms, organizing and running community school visitations, and planning graduation exercises.[43] One of the main areas that the PTA

99

contributed to was the physical education program. Raising funds to provide for football, baseball, and basketball uniforms became one of their immediate goals, as well as organizing a Young America Club. Later they helped provide instruments for the school band and funded the elaborate and long running school newspaper.

Local businesses pitched in to supply materials and support the school effort. Sponsoring the school newspaper on a regular basis was: The Round-Up, McCarthy's Cafe, Southern Barbecue, Red- ding Creamery Products, Summit City Men's Clothing, and Phetteplace Store.[44] Pioneering entrepreneurs Leland Kronschnable and Wynn Price raised money to keep Central Valley Elementary School supplied. This kind of community action proved to be especially important when the Shasta County Planning Commission ruled that placing permanent school buildings in the dam area would be a mistake. The commission stated that transient and migratory dam workers would only be staying for a 3-4 year period. After a lively verbal exchange with concerned dam area citizens, the commission voted to supply only portable classrooms and a minimum of supplies.[45]

Lacking money and supplies, many school related student activities centered around enjoying the outdoors and playing simple games. Years later, residents recalled these years as youngsters with many fond memories (Bureau of Reclamation).

The early church movement in the Shasta Dam area contributed only little toward fostering community participation. Traditionally, as in the case with colonial New England and early eighteenth century "burned over district" of New York, the church membership and community involvement became synonymous. Yet, dam workers in the early Depression era had never attended church in large numbers or used the institution as a major source of rallying community action. This trend continued at the Shasta Dam site, where the few churches that were started had a difficult time keeping congregation membership up.

Snowfall fell regularly in the far end of the Sacramento Valley during the boomtown years, and when it came, children lost no time in getting out, building snowmen and throwing snowballs at unsuspecting friends (Bureau of Reclamation).

The first two years of boomtown growth (1938-39) saw only three small churches inaugurated. The Methodist Home Mission organization sent Miss Grace Kendrick to initiate and preside over a Central Valley Methodist Church. Bringing some funds with her and with money donated by local businesses and patrons, Kendrick persuaded Redding ministers to commute to the fledgling church and deliver sermons.[46] Early services generated scant crowds in a half-completed building, yet those who did participate formed a strong bond that helped many still unemployed families hang on through difficult months ahead.[47] In September of 1938 local Summit City residents finished construction of The First Baptist Church. Reverend F. A. Burks attempted to increase the meager membership with a house-to-house campaign. He received few new members and little in the way of donations.[48] Burks' most successful activity centered on his ongoing Sunday school program, where numerous children participated on a regular basis. It appears that boomtown adults felt that it was important for their children to receive regular religious training, while they themselves did not. Residents claimed to have had deep religious convictions. They simply had learned to live without attending regular church services.

One of the most popular annual events included the "Miss Lake" beauty pageant. Always well attended, this "contest" offered any boomtown female the opportunity to gain area-wide recognition and a small monetary prize (Bureau of Reclamation).

The first Catholic services in the area occurred on September 12, 1938 in a Central Valley dance hall. Father A. T. Gavin, of Redding's St. Joseph Church presided over an initial congregation of fifty, children included.[49] Attendance in this church, as well as the other two, remained at low levels until after World War II.

All of the churches encouraged community participation in developing an improved lifestyle. From the earliest days, all three churches ran successful food and shelter programs. These community drives were particularly active during religious holidays, when even nonmembers gave generously to those families not yet enjoying the income from dam employment. The Central Valley Methodist Church determined to muster a local scout troop that, at one point, boasted scores of local children, and still survives till this day.[50]

Boomtown women donated hundreds of hours at the Toyon Day Care Community center (shown above). Just like their male counterparts, the hardships of the times found women developing close ties with others in their community (Bureau of Reclamation).

Women also joined local pep clubs in impressive numbers and met on a bi-weekly basis to discuss everything from world events to tips on saving money. At these meetings, women socialized and worked diligently on quilts and afghan blankets. Close personal relationships developed that, over the years, linked friends together in the difficult war years ahead. To Adah Hubbard, charter member of the Central Valley Pep Club, the clubs provided relief from the everyday pressures of keeping house under trying conditions.[51] The local boomtown pep clubs organized dozens of social events every year. Most activities centered on raising money for some local cause or providing opportunities for people to get to know each other. In this way, one can say that these clubs aided greatly in building a positive community spirit, one that encouraged participation from everyone.

An example of social mixing was evident in the schools and in their PTA's. It has already been shown that Toyon School served students from the Government Camp, the Contractor's Camp, Summit City, Project City, and Central Valley. Numerous articles from the school newspaper refer to new relationships developed by youngsters living in different towns. In many cases, students would ride the bus to a friend's home in order to play after school.[52] The local PTA meetings mixed hundreds of residents, and bridge, pinochle, whist, and other card game clubs were spawned from early meetings.[53]

The Bureau of Reclamation encouraged socializing at its newly constructed community hall at Toyon. Dances, fund raising events, club meetings, and holiday parties all took place here throughout the period of dam building. Residents from all the boomtowns attended along with numerous others from Redding and small towns in Shasta County. Acquaintances made at the Toyon center continued over into family friendships that have extended down to today.

Inter-community events such as safety and production awards ceremonies sponsored by the Bureau of Reclamation helped increase awareness of the many diverse jobs at the construction site, and the people doing those jobs. In the photograph above, a worker is honored for his quick thinking in helping another worker injured at the dam (Bureau of Reclamation).

104

Individual boomtowns also encouraged the development of a homogeneous society. As early as December of 1938 Summit City organized a huge Christmas celebration complete with a forty-foot Christmas tree setup in the middle of town. Local businessmen provided leadership and funds to feature a special Christmas dinner and dance. Door-to-door canvassing brought out even the most recalcitrant residents.[54] Not to be outdone, boomtown and Toyon leaders by December of 1939 planned and enjoyed their own Christmas festivities. It was not unusual for residents of one town to partake in the holiday activities of one or more of the adjoining towns. Many residents interviewed stated that these holiday parties brought people closer together and helped foster open communication between the boomtowns.

Socializing between towns was not restricted to holiday affairs. Several levels of interaction involved almost everyone in ongoing relationships. From children at Toyon, and later Central Valley School to high school students bussed to Shasta High School in Redding, young people readily accepted this forced integration. On another level, women resolved to build social connections that would help them deal with the harsh physical conditions evident in starting a new town. Many women, particularly those without children whose husbands worked a six-day work week, had to deal with loneliness. Pep clubs, card clubs, sewing groups, and the PTA allowed women to gather on a regular basis to have companionship and swap tips on shopping and running the household. Membership was open to any interested woman. Wives of government inspectors would sew quilts and organize fund-raisers right alongside construction "stiffs" wives.

On the job too, white-collared government inspectors would often make friends with PCI supervisors and blue-collared cement workers, and socialize with them during off hours.[55] One of the most popular forms of socializing was in sports. Local boomtowns supported teams in baseball, football, and basketball. While schedules called for action against towns around the entire county, competition was most keen whenever the boomtown baseball teams played each other. Interestingly enough, membership on the Toyon team did not require residence at the government camp. Several team members resided in Central Valley and Summit City.

On another level, male socializing was most obvious at the many beer halls, nightclubs, and dance halls lining Shasta Dam Blvd. and Kennett Road. Here, on a nightly basis, dam workers met, drank, gambled, and just plain had a good time. While a considerable number of fights and disturbances occurred, usually over gambling, for the most part tavern-type socializing initiated strong personal relationships that have endured the test of time. Music, beer, and cards became the accepted environment for hours of social interaction. Many of the beer halls advertised family entertainment, and encouraged female participation.[56]

The hardships of their jobs naturally drove dam workers to seek relaxation in the many saloon, beer halls and card clubs sprinkled throughout the boomtown area. As these business establishments sought patronage expansion, their owners encouraged workers to bring in "the wife and kids" (Bureau of Reclamation).

Socializing between families occurred on a much more frequent and regular schedule than it does today. It became important for families to visit each other, usually on regularly scheduled days. Many surviving dam workers have pointed to this phenomenon as one of the main social differences apparent today. The usual scenario involved one family inviting the other over for dinner, usually a barbecue. For adults, card playing and casual conversation followed dinner. Many times, particularly near payday, families would meet at one of the many boomtown diners or restaurants. After their meal, the families would enjoy a movie at the Shasta Theatre or go to the skating rink, or the bowling alley. Families, every once in awhile, would make the trip into Redding usually for shopping.

For many dam workers their life consisted of focused, hard work on the job, and enjoying family and friends in the evenings and on the weekends. Few of them, traveled further than Redding; during the Depression gas was available, but most did not spend what little cash they had on "pleasure driving". Later, during World War II, gas rationing severely limited automobile travel to "necessary destinations" (Bureau of Reclamation).

While economic homogeneity may have been present and applicable to the majority of boomtown residents, it by no means indicates that social harmony prevailed. In fact, some residents clearly indicate that a de facto class distinction did exist. One area of dispute about the homogeneity of the population centered on the relationship between the government personnel and other boomtown residents. On one hand, men like hard working dungaree-dirty Ray Rogers complained that a feeling of segregation existed between Toyon residents and the "rest of us."[57] He neither socialized with government inspectors nor frequented homes in Toyon, preferring to mix with boomtown neighbors or PCI employees. Using the term "elitists," Rogers recalled that few of the "government men" frequented the beer halls in Central Valley.

Ralph Lowry, shown above addressing a mixed crowd of dam workers and their families modeled community involvement between Toyon engineers and residents of the boomtowns. He approved a wide variety of "social events" at the Toyon Community Center; the events encouraged family attendance for any local residents (Bureau of Reclamation).

Rogers' statements however are, disputed by Harold Fortier, a government inspector. Fortier stated that he and other Toyon residents spent many hours socializing in boomtown establishments. Fortier claims that many boomtown friends visited and socialized in his Toyon home, and that he reciprocated by visiting them.[58] Loral Butcher, a former dam worker, sided with Fortier claiming that many "government people" socialized with boomtown residents. He remembered however, that few of his friends lived in Toyon.[59] Bob Sass, another dam worker and Central Valley resident provides still another viewpoint. He stated that unmarried government personnel did in fact shun social relationships in the boomtowns, preferring entertainment in Redding. Married men living in Toyon, particularly those who had wives that made friendships within the boomtowns tended to socialize there.[60]

Bureau of Reclamation administration building dominated the frontage road scene for any driver going from the boomtowns to the dam site. Dam workers and family members recalled a feeling of "openness" and "friendliness" whenever visiting the dormitories, homes or community center (Bureau of Reclamation).

One interesting interpretation on homogeneity came from Pete Forte, Central Valley resident and dam worker. Forte had lived in Boulder City as his father worked on Boulder Dam, and he remembered everyone living "quite close" where government men, contractors, and construction stiffs were "almost forced to mix and get along." Homes within Boulder City were not segregated into class sections and blue-collar workers lived next door to federal inspectors.[61] He claimed that the physical isolation of Toyon and Shasta Dam Village (contractor's camp) helped to induce some social segregation. Yet, he added, that for the most part, a homogeneous social environment prevailed. He himself had numerous friends in both Toyon and Shasta Dam Village. Reinforcing this opinion is Walter Kuehne, a Minnesota migrant and Central Valley resident. Kuehne recalled little evidence of an elitist attitude by government workers or of self-imposed segregation. He vividly remembered that mixing and socializing between the residents of the dam towns was commonplace and regular. He added that a strong feeling of community spirit permeated most households in every town.[62]

109

It appears that the homogeneity issue can best be understood when interpreted as a self-selecting process. One common trend that nearly all the interviewed persons referred to was the fact that they socialized with families that they had selected, not necessarily those living the nearest. Men tended to initiate relationships with other men that they had either worked with on previous dam jobs or that they now worked with. These initial acquaintanceships usually expanded to include the wives and children of each family, and over a period of time developed into close relationships that, in numerous cases, withstood many years.

By 1940, the national news media (radio and newspaper) sent journalists to the Shasta Dam construction site regularly. In the photograph above, Ralph Lowry, Bureau engineer (right) is "interviewed." Notice that both the journalist and Lowry are reading from a pre-approved government script (Bureau of Reclamation).

Chapter 8
The Impact of Redding and World War II

From the earliest days in 1937, the fledgling boomtowns relied on the support services of Redding. These support services helped create an inviting social and economic environment that encouraged Shasta Dam area residents to build permanent communities. Whereas stability had developed from the beginning in Boulder City where the government created and sustained a complete residential and commercial support environment, the Shasta Dam boomtowns struggled to become established. Both Toyon and Shasta Dam Village provided little in the way of social and economic assistance. It was Redding, already somewhat of a regional center for the immediate North Valley area, that would funnel goods and services into the rapidly developing boomtowns. For the years 1937-1945 the Shasta Dam area rose to become the primary delivery and interaction zone within Redding's nodal region.[1]

Nodality, a geographic and economic term used to determine the spatial relationship between people and goods, can be measured to discover the amount of influence a dominant regional center has over newly developing outlying communities.[2] Contact between a central service center and a developing urban hinterland usually occurs along prescribed routes of least resistance. Brian Berry, an urban geographer interested in the diffusion of goods and services between urban nodal centers, argued that one of the first signs of increased contact between a newly forming community and an already established city is improved transportation routes.[3] As has already been shown, boomtown development occurred along roads, Highway 99 and Kennett-Buckeye Road. With the initiation of the first residential and commercial buildings, boomtown pioneers pleaded and worked for improving both routes with the hope that better transportation links would increase social and economic support from Redding.

Residents recalled the importance of Redding's greater variety of goods and services and its importance, particularly in the early years. Loral Butcher, a Central Valley resident, remembered that, "all of my friends and myself would go into Redding for our serious shopping."[4] He stated that furniture and clothing stores with variety were not available in the boomtowns. George Van Eaton, Toyon resident, agreed with Butcher. He recalled that his family drove into Redding for "most of my purchases."[5] One of the biggest shopping attractions in Redding during this time was the, warehouse-like department store of McCormick-Seltzer. Locally owned and operated, the McCormick-Seltzer Store offered low prices and the largest variety of dry goods north of Sacramento. On payday, wives of dam workers eagerly made the ten-mile trip from the boomtowns to Redding. While in town it was not unusual for them to shop many hours at McCormick-Seltzer and other clothing and department stores.

The McCormick-Seltzer store retained an excellent reputation for high quality dry goods and groceries. The family owned store traced its roots back into the late nineteenth century (Shasta Historical Society).

Entertainment opportunities in Redding brought in boomtown residents on a regular basis. California Street became the favorite off-time hangout for dozens of unmarried dam workers. Stretching for several blocks along California Street taverns, dance halls, and beer halls thrived. Larger, noisier, and boasting of more action than their smaller boomtown counterparts, they swelled to capacity on Friday and Saturday nights.

Lonely dam workers often had dinner, went to a movie, and socialized in a favorite tavern on a regular basis. Many of these "regulars" formed close-knit social groups that maintained friendships both on the job and off.

The Cascade Theater provided one of the few opportunities to view first-run Hollywood movies. Boomtown residents usually saved weekend visits to Redding for "dinner and a movie" (Shasta Historical Society).

Families too, found the attraction of Redding difficult to resist. Shopping, dinner, and the movies topped the list as "the things" to do. Boomtown women and children especially looked forward to a fun time in "the city." Opal Foxx remembered friends telling her that boomtown conditions were so primitive in 1937 and 1938 that a trip into Redding was more of a necessity than a luxury.[6] As time went on, however, and as the boomtowns continued to grow, dam workers and their families made less frequent trips. They reserved shopping in Redding for special items such as hard to find appliances, special services, and the purchasing of automobiles.

In terms of secondary education, Redding served as a regional link. The Shasta County Schools Office located in town provided materials and valuable support services to rural schools like Toyon. The only high school in the area was Shasta High School, and all of the boomtown 9th-12th grade students were bussed to Redding. PCI donated funds to add a new wing of classrooms at Shasta High School to accommodate the hundreds of new students. Boomtown students at Shasta remembered the initial difficulty they had in being accepted socially. Known as the "son of a dam(n) worker" or called "poor white trash" a few students felt outside the mainstream of their graduating class.[7] Minor incidents such as these passed within a couple of years, and by the beginning of World War II most students felt comfortable and accepted.

Shasta High School's impressive new buildings drew in secondary students from all around the county. The road running horizontally in front of the school is Eureka Way (Shasta Historical Society).

Redding provided much of the necessary financial support that boomtown homeowners and business leaders desperately needed. Banks and savings & loans did not come to the boomtowns during the early years and this forced boomtown residents to seek help in Redding. A natural

114

consequence of the Great Depression was the lack of available cash to fund mortgages and new businesses. Cash was difficult to come by and loans were always a risk during this economic downturn. Numerous boomtown residents felt the economic pinch when refused credit in Redding. Harsh feelings surfaced after several unfortunate incidents at banking establishments. Already disturbed by the continuing use of derogatory remarks such as "dam(n) people," "Okies," "Arkies," and "winos," and then the refusal of credit, some boomtown residents made fewer and fewer trips into Redding.[8] Butcher recalled a visit to a local Redding bank in which he was turned down for a mortgage loan. Butcher questioned the refusal and the bank supervisor replied that the loan would only be approved if Butcher could provide a $6000 cash collateral, the amount of the loan itself.[9]

Downtown Redding during the late 1930s effectively evolved into the commercial hub of the northstate. By this time, paved roads radiated outward in all directions, particularly south to Sacramento and north to Oregon (Shasta Historical Society).

As Redding provided a necessary source of social and economic security to the boomtowns, so did the boomtowns and the dam work rejuvenate Redding's economy. Redding and Shasta County had wallowed

115

in an economic depression ever since the copper boom played-out after World War I. Bureau of Reclamation personnel, who had first established an office in Redding, began spending federal funds in early 1938. As large scale hiring began by the summer of the same year Redding businesspersons hoped for a business upturn. By the end of December of 1938, business sales volumes had doubled from the previous year. Redding merchants proudly pointed to increased revenues ranging from 40% to 300%. In every case, all existing and new businesses prospered. When asked about their new success, local businesspersons attributed the boom to dam construction work.[10] A local survey revealed that dam working customers were spending considerable money on luxuries (e.g., radios, electric appliances). The previous year most people purchased only food, clothing, and other necessary items.

During the Depression years and on into World War II, Coca-Cola maintain high popularity in Shasta County. The bottling company shown above made regular trips to the boomtown area's stores and restaurants to deliver the "classic bottle" (Shasta Historical Society).

A merchandising expert reporting for a local newspaper told readers that in nearly every instance seasonal stocks of goods had been sold-out by Christmas (1938). He further commented that few stores would have to

116

"unload" remaining stock. In the same paper the United States Postal Service reported that postal receipts had reached an all-time high.[11]

New construction and people moving into Redding reached "boom proportions" by the end of 1938.[12] The population of Redding doubled from just over 4,000 in 1930 to over 8,000 by the end of 1939. New electric meters, an indication of completed homes, were installed at a feverish pace as 417 meters went into operation for the year. Building valuations passed the one million dollar mark for the first time in Redding's history, and it was noted in local newspapers that most of the construction was directly related to the Shasta Dam project.[13] In the commercial sector, 56 new businesses applied for permits within the city limits, and the county planning commission reported that traffic had doubled on the city streets.[14] The boom can best be understood in terms of the money paid for over 19 million man-hours of work. Much of this federal money was spent in Redding.

Boulder City, a "planned city," supported engineers and workers in building mighty Boulder (Hoover) Dam in the early 1930s. Some of these workers, actually, hundreds of them, migrated to the Shasta Dam area later—living in one of the boomtowns or Toyon (Bureau of Reclamation).

Redding was to the Shasta boomtowns what Las Vegas was to the Boulder City. With the government's announcement of the Hoover Dam project, speculation soared and business exploded. The population of Las Vegas, like Redding, doubled in a short period of time (1931-1934), as did new registered business starts. Gambling was legalized the same year that building began and casinos soon dotted the downtown area.[15] Highway 95 provided the Boulder City dam workers quick access to the shopping and entertainment advantages found in nearby Las Vegas, much in the same manner that Highway 99 linked Redding and the boomtowns. Las Vegas supplied Boulder City residents with basic supplies, hard to find merchandise, and a full range of entertainment. Besides the infamous "gambling, boozing, and playing" prevalent in the downtown district, Las Vegas businesses realized a regular clientele interested in household luxuries such as radios and washing machines.[16] The comparison with Redding is justifiable and readily apparent. Both Redding and Las Vegas grew quickly and profitably to the point where they established themselves as regional service centers during the dam building years.

Pete Forte, a resident of Boulder City and Central Valley, remembered the growth attributed to Las Vegas and Redding. Forte recalled Las Vegas in 1931 as looking very similar to the way Redding looked in 1937. Then as dam construction moved ahead, both towns exploded in residential and commercial growth. He admitted that Las Vegas and Redding both served as necessary social and economic support centers for the newly forming dam boomtowns. In turn, dam activity, in the form of people and money, encouraged and promoted an expanded commercial center in Las Vegas and Redding.[17]

Many new job opportunities opened up during the dam building years. Boomtown residents, both men and women, took advantage of advertised positions and applied for jobs as diesel and truck mechanics, office and clerical secretaries, and skilled workers in the mechanical trades.[18] These early instances of dam area residents employed in Redding foreshadowed a larger, more economically impacting phenomenon that occurred after World War II, where hundreds of former dam workers held jobs outside the boomtown area. Historians Robert Wiley, Robert Gottlieb, and Gerald Nash have all stressed the social and economic impact of World War II on the American West. The global conflict initiated a tremendous social and economic transformation. Over two million workers poured into California, creating urban boomtowns that easily surpassed the size and intensity of the dam boomtowns. New job opportunities during World War II, particularly in aircraft and shipbuilding, impacted the lives of the Shasta Dam workers. Richmond, California, for example, expanded rapidly from 23,000 persons to over 115,000 as Henry Kaiser set up one of the country's largest shipyards.[19] Meanwhile, further south, the Navy town of San Diego doubled its population as it became regional headquarters for Naval and Marine units stationed in the Pacific. Los Angeles, likewise, grew tremendously with the expansion of aircraft factories and other war industries.

Historian Gary Nash reminded us of the importance of the aircraft industry during the war years on California employment. Over 60 percent of all federal monies expended in California went to building military aircraft. Most of the activity, centered in southern California, boasted more than 300,000 workers by 1945.[20] They worked in huge new plants especially constructed to produce assembly line aircraft. Factory plants of such firms as Douglas, Lockheed, North American, Northrop, Hughes, Convair, and Ryan employed thousands of men and women in an intense effort to mass-produce airplanes and other weapons of war. The incentive for workers included good pay and special bonuses for surpassing production quotas.

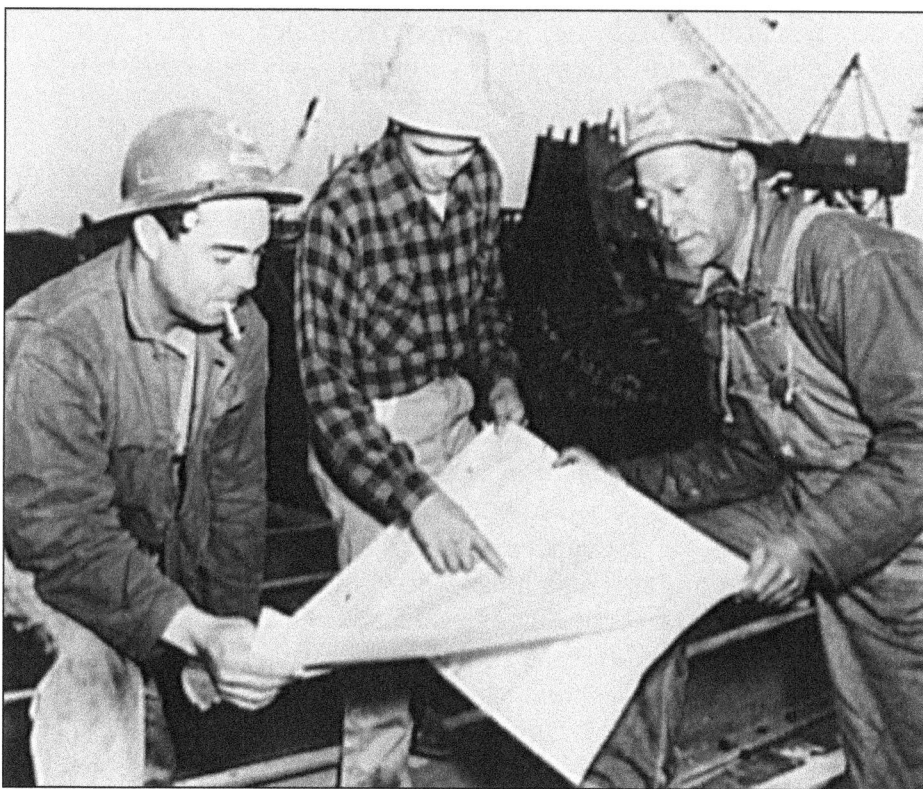

Beginning in mid-1942 and continuing for most the war years, Shasta Dam workers fled the hot summers and moderate pay of dam work, to join the tens of thousands of war workers laboring in the Kaiser Shipyards. The work proved just as dangerous, but higher pay rates swayed hundreds of workers to move south (Bureau of Reclamation).

Of nearly the same magnitude was the shipbuilding effort that centered around the San Francisco Bay Area. Henry Kaiser led the industry

119

with over four billion dollars in federal shipbuilding contracts. Companies such as Todd Shipbuilding Corporation and Bethlehem Shipbuilding along with Kaiser employed thousands in plants at Richmond, Oakland, Sausalito, and Vallejo.[21] As in the aircraft industry, salary levels and job security attracted men and women from all over the state and the country.

Hundreds of Shasta Dam workers earning between $.75 and $1.25 an hour left their dam work and moved to the Bay Area or Los Angeles where hourly rates had surpassed these levels by mid- 1941. Firm figures are not available for those who left, but accounts from boomtown residents who remained behind estimated that the number was between 1,000 and 2,000 workers and their families. They left Shasta County either to serve in the military or to work in war-related industries.[22] Many of those that left were skilled workers. They realized that their training and experience could command greater wages in the shipyards or aircraft factories.

The composition of the work force at Shasta Dam changed considerably during World War II. Many of the skilled workers at the dam site were able to acquire deferments from military service when the federal government listed Shasta Dam as an important defense project. The expected power generated from Shasta Dam was needed in the Bay Area, as was controlled water supplies for the numerous large farms in the Sacramento River Valley. The deferments however, applied only to "key" personnel, usually highly skilled workers, managers, supervisors, inspectors, and engineers. Scores of boomtown men enlisted and/or were drafted by early 1942, and a labor shortage at the dam appeared imminent.[23] To fill the gap left by those leaving for better paying jobs and/or military service, PCI supervisors and Bureau representatives conceived the idea of bussing in new help. For the most part, the employment roundup concentrated in the Sacramento, Bay Area, Los Angeles, and Portland areas. Jobless men, usually of very low skills, were "recruited" and brought into the boomtown area. Of the hundreds of men driven to the area, about half refused the dangerous and unfamiliar work.[24] The others moved into the boomtowns as the latest contingent of residents.

In an attempt to keep as many skilled workers as possible, PCI voluntarily raised wages approximately 50%. AFL union representatives approved of the raise and a large number of workers who were considering changing jobs decided to stay. For many the reason for staying involved their perception that Shasta County was a great place to live. Hearing stories, mostly true, of incredibly crowded and inadequate housing conditions in the Bay Area and Los Angeles, boomtown residents saw benefits in Shasta's relatively quiet and safe environment. In addition, many of the dam workers had moved numerous times during the Depression, and they were just plain tired of relocating. For some, it had been 10- 12 years since they had settled down in a permanent home situation. Over half of the workers now had young children, and they wanted a stable home in a good environment. Workers also decided to stay when it was learned that the number of overtime shifts would be increased. The government needed the expected power immediately, as military reversals in the Pacific pressured the American war effort. The standard forty hour work week made up of 6.65 hour shifts remained, yet, work now continued every day, in all types of weather, including snow.[25]

In describing the demographic situation at the boomtowns during the global war residents noticed a much greater fluidity as men and families moved out of the area about as fast as new ones were moving in. Walter Kuehne came out to the boomtowns from Minnesota when he had been told that there were good jobs available. Kuehne arrived with his entire family in the early part of1942, quickly set up household and began work at the dam.[26] Leonard Groves, dam worker and boomtown resident, recalled that most of the men who left the area were quite young, while older workers remained. These older workers and their families had already made the decision that the Shasta Dam area would be their permanent homes. The war helped them to reinforce this decision. As they read the news and talked to friends about the uncertainty of the future, more and more of the workers came to realize that now was the time to "settle down" and make the best of the wartime conditions.[27]

The most extreme example of this desire to stay in the Shasta Dam area was revealed by Walter Kuehne when he told of a friend, a young draftee who flunked his army induction medical exam by pretending to "hear voices." The worker returned to Central Valley, where he promptly resumed his dam working duties.[28]

Another important impact of World War II on the boomtowns occurred to house prices in the area. All through 1942 home prices nose-dived as the number of workers leaving Shasta County exceeded those moving in. Homes in the $300 to $500 price range fell to as low as $100. Business also decreased as the original boomtown economic conditions eased. Some local entrepreneurs, like early pioneer Rudi Raki, felt insecure in this period of unsettled economic conditions. He closed down his previously successful ice cream shop, The Big Dipper, and moved out of the area. Raki, like many others, would return to the Shasta Dam area after the war, reopening businesses.[29] The local bowling alley also shut down along with several beer and dance halls. However, during the war years, several new businesses opened. Watching the continued prosperity of the boomtowns' only movie house the, Shasta Theatre, local entrepreneurs gambled by opening a second theatre, the Mecca. It would last for only a short time.[30]

Wartime conditions tended to encourage isolation between the boomtown communities, Toyon, and Shasta Dam Village. First and foremost was the nationwide gas rationing program that limited pleasure driving. Even though the Shasta Dam project had been given a AA-1 defense rating, and therefore priority on supplies such as gasoline, only certain "key" personnel obtained the "C" sticker, allowing them a larger portion of fuel. In any event, the gasoline was to be used by workers to facilitate their official duties, and most workers appeared to have honored this responsibility.[31]

The physical layout of the Shasta Dam area boomtowns did not encourage close contact between communities and without the extensive use of the automobile many residents remained isolated during the war. Walking between Project City and Central Valley occurred to some degree, since these two towns were relatively close at one mile. However, a walk from the contractor's camp at Shasta Dam Village to the nearest boomtown of Summit City was over three miles, and all uphill. Toyon residents could walk to Summit City but few ventured out to journey on foot to Central Valley, Project City, or to Shasta Dam Village. There were no sidewalks on Shasta Dam Blvd. or on Kennett Road, and these roads were somewhat dangerous due to heavy truck traffic.

Patriotic responses to the gas rationing regulations sustained a high level of participation during World War II in Shasta County. At least that is how many boomtown residents replied to the question about travel inconveniences during this time. One resident stated, "We just saved up our trips" (Library of Congress).

It did not take long for the call to go out for women workers—at Shasta Dam and elsewhere in the area. By mid-1942 women worked as clerks (payroll, filing, typing) in the Bureau office or as a telephone receptionist, as shown above (Bureau of Reclamation).

To compensate for this lack of mobility during World War II, residents engaged in fewer trips concerned with social and economic errands. Workers and their families shopped only once or twice a week, usually combining these trips with a visit to friends living in other towns. In addition, jaunts into Redding were also reduced and dam workers came to regard a trip into Redding as a highlight of the week or even the month.[32] With the increased isolation between towns residents began to explore their own neighborhoods more. Evidence, from interviews, indicated that new relationships developed between previously unacquainted neighbors. Walking around their neighborhoods, residents began to meet new friends and began to shop in more of their local stores. Women in particular developed neighborhood clubs aimed at supporting the war effort, but also to satisfy the now difficult to achieve inter-town social contact dominant before the war.

All of the boomtowns, in an effort to achieve more mobility during the war, established carpooling systems. The system became so pervasive that violators were quickly identified and admonished, both at the official level, and by other residents.[33] By mid-1942, at the height of Japanese advances in the Pacific, concern reached a peak. Flat tires were patched over and over again instead of replacing them and residents conserved gasoline as intently as ever. In at least one way the carpooling system encouraged new and closer relationships. Neighbors came to depend on each other for hard to get items and for seat space in automobiles. To this end contact increased between households as everyone made a concerted effort to coordinate activities.

During the war new work opportunities opened up for the women of the Shasta Dam area boomtowns. Whereas before the war, few women were employed by the Bureau of Reclamation or Pacific Constructors, more and more joined the payrolls as hundreds of men left for military service or higher paying jobs in the shipyards and aircraft plants of the Bay Area and Southern California. Toyon School, by 1944 lost its last remaining male teacher and even Shasta High School dramatically changed its male-female teacher ratio.[34] Pacific Constructors hired many women to work in clerical positions and in the kitchen/mess hail. Opal Foxx came out from Kansas in January of 1942 to see relatives working on the dam. At that time only men worked for the company. She and several others applied for and were hired to work in the coffee shop and later in the main mess hall. Her mess hall job consisted of washing dishes for the swing shift. She worked six days a week from 6p.m. till 2 a.m. and received $3.20 for an eight hour shift.[35] Within seven months, Foxx transferred to the day shift as relief-cook at the mess hall. As this job paid much better than her previous dish washing position,

Foxx was determined to make a go of it. This proved difficult as soon she was informed that it had always been a tradition to use only male cooks at the mess hail. She also learned that a female cook would portend bad luck for all those around her if she continued. Undaunted, Foxx proceeded to gain the respect of her male counterparts by cutting up two crates of cabbages in record time using only a French carving knife. Amazed and bewildered male cooks, who had always used a large slicing machine to cut up cabbage, quickly accepted Foxx and she remained on the job till the end of the war.[36]

The woman shown here, is distributing a food ration booklet to a registered Boulder City resident. Although unlawful at the time, residents openly talked about "trading stamps" for their favorite foods (Library of Congress).

The area of largest opportunity for women appeared in the clerical field. In Redding and boomtown businesses, and in the offices of the Bureau of Reclamation and Pacific Constructors, women assumed typing and filing positions. In the Bureau of Reclamation Office at Toyon, at least a dozen women assumed clerical roles by 1943 and the number increased by 1945.[37] More and more women also hired on at boomtown businesses, either helping their husbands, or in some cases taking over the family business while their husbands served overseas. Vivian Jencks assisted her husband at the Donut Hole in Project City and June Murphy took on full cashier duties at Murphy's Grocery Store also in Project City.[38] In Central Valley the Shasta Theatre, the Central Valley Skating Rink, Pike's Market, and other businesses hired women during the war. In Redding, the local Office of Price Administration (OPA) assembled dozens of women to handle the distribution of war coupons and government information.

The war brought great changes in community cooperation, much of it organized and run by women. Scrap roundups became a daily affair for action oriented club groups in the boomtowns. Newspapers, rubber, iron, and almost every reusable substance was recycled. Women led the war bond drives by sponsoring events that encouraged participation. Local clubs shared war news and helped console the relatives of those who lost loved ones in combat action. Women at the contractor's camp also involved themselves in the war effort. They organized active committees for Red Cross sewing and knitting. Their Home Nursing courses became popular with women throughout the boomtowns.[39]

Boomtown residents dealt with higher prices throughout the war years. Prices on many items rose 20% to 30% for foods such as cheese, meat, and coffee.[40] To match the increased prices of consumer products, wages also increased. Wages rose from an average of $.99 an hour to an average of $1.60 by war's end.[41]

While never more than a handful of blacks worked on Shasta Dam, dozens of Mexicans were brought in to fill the work gap created by exiting dam workers. Mexicans trucked in from as far away as Los Angeles assumed working positions in menial low skill jobs. It is not clear whether these Mexican migrants were invited up to work on Shasta Dam or forced through government efforts. After some initial objection by local labor union leaders, the Mexicans were able to obtain temporary membership privileges. This resulted mainly due to efforts by Bureau leaders and reinforced by the original government contract with PCI that called for all work on the dam to be done by union members.[42] Little is known about these Mexican workers except that they worked well despite preconceived notions of laziness on the part of white workers. Their social experience during off duty hours is a mystery. No mention is made of them in the PCI official dam book Shasta Dam and Its Builders and surviving residents do not remember much about them.

"Everything changed," remarked one ex-dam worker, when asked about the impact of World War II on their boomtown lifestyle. Most clearly remembered proved to be a strong sense of "togetherness"—that the work on Shasta Dam really contributed to the war effort (Bureau of Reclamation).

Chapter 9
The Postwar Years, 1945-1950

Stabilization of the Shasta Dam boomtowns occurred between the years 1945 and 1950. A number of economic factors rejuvenated the local economy just as thousands of workers were completing their jobs on Shasta Dam. Foremost among these new economic factors, the lumber boom, initiated the hiring of thousands of loggers, saw mill operators, logging truck drivers, and lumber yard workers. Maintenance and finishing work at Shasta Dam continued to employ hundreds as well as related government water and power projects. Lastly, the city of Redding, entering a post World War II stage of economic expansion, began to offer new employment opportunities in the retail and service related fields.

The diversion of lumber to war-related projects during World War II created a domestic housing shortage that became acute with the end of hostilities and the return of millions of GI's. Redding assumed the role as a regional center for the processing of timber and the transportation of finished wood products. Timber cut in northern Shasta County and nearby Siskiyou, Lassen, and Trinity Counties was trucked to dozens of new sawmills in and around Redding that opened between 1945 and 1950. Several large mills opened at Burney, some 50 miles to the east of Redding, and in Anderson, ten miles south of Redding. Shasta Dam area men obtained positions at these lumber mills and commuted to work via an improved road system.

Highway 299, winding its way through rugged mountain terrain, had been difficult to maintain, particularly during the winter snows. During World War II, however, the road was repaved and plowed often. This enabled timber from the Burney-MacAruthur Falls area to be shipped out on a regular basis in support of the war effort. As the postwar lumber boom grew additional state funds helped to rework a particularly hazardous 14 mile section of Highway 299 on Hatchet Mountain.[1] The same highway was also improved as it headed west out of Redding toward Eureka. The previously narrow winding road, treacherous in the winter months, forced state officials to widen and repave much of the 100 mile section through the coast ranges. In addition, state highway commissioners, with the continual urging and financial assistance of the federal government, reworked portions of north-south running Highway 99.

The above-mentioned highways and numerous new county roads allowed boomtown residents to secure lumber jobs within a new commuting system. The Scott Lumber Mill, Peterson and Vogt Mill, Indian Head Lumber Company, and the Toutsch Sawmill Company, all clustered around Burney, offered jobs. Most of the boomtown men who worked in these mills, either commuted daily or lived in company housing and commuted home to Central Valley on the weekends. By 1950 the Scott Lumber Mill alone employed over 300 men, many of them ex-dam workers.[2]

Wilbur Smith, ex-dam worker, recalled that gasoline became readily available as wartime gas rationing ended. He also noted that most dam workers had, by 1950, one or two automobiles and that most Central Valley residents "drove to work in the neighboring lumber mills."[3]

The largest number of boomtown commuters drove to the huge newly built lumber mills of Anderson. This tiny town, located just south of Redding, grew quickly in 1948 with the establishment of Shasta Plywood (later U. S. Plywood). The plant, gigantic by local comparisons, had been designed to produce Novoply (particle board), a new compressed wood product that held promise for residential wall construction. Its immediate popularity allowed U. S. Plywood to expand building new plants across the country. Redding plant manager, Gene Brewer, utilizing new technology and expertise from hundreds of former dam workers, who now worked at the plant, rose to become the company's president. Brewer believed, correctly, that the accumulated knowledge and experience of Shasta Dam workers could be of a great benefit to his company in terms of adapting existing wood processing techniques to new large scale assembly line production methods that had been utilized successfully during dam construction.[4]

Returning veterans, such as Bob Heikka, found employment at U. S. Plywood. He continued to commute the sixteen miles from Central Valley to the wood plant for thirty-six years.[5] Walter Kuehne, a resident of the postwar boomtown area and ex-dam worker, recalled that "scores of his friends" worked at the Anderson plywood plants commuting daily, many times carpooling.[6] Ray Rogers, a foreman at Shasta Dam and the smaller Keswick Dam (located nearby), remembered large numbers of dam workers "transferring" to positions at U. S. Plywood. Rogers kept concise records on his personnel, and he recalled that in 1949 alone 120 of his men moved on to jobs in Anderson. Most of these men continued to live in the boomtown area, preferring to commute to work.[7] Another former dam worker who secured employment in the Anderson wood mills was Bob Foxx. Foxx finished his work on the dam in the summer of 1945 and he applied to the

Bureau of Reclamation for work on additional water projects. He succeeded in finding employment for several months on nearby Keswick Dam, only to be bumped from the position by returning World War II veterans. Foxx then applied for and was hired at Shasta Plywood, where he continued to work until his death thirty years later.[8]

The Novoply wood processing plant (United States Plywood Company) provided steady employment for hundreds of post-World War II workers. This plant, located in Anderson spurred the opening of additional lumber mills (Shasta Historical Society).

At this same time, 1948, Ralph L. Smith Lumber Company began hiring hundreds of men in a nearby wood processing plant in Anderson. Later this large processing plant would be bought-out by Kimberly-Clark and expanded to become one of the largest wood processing plants on the west coast. As was the case with U. S. Plywood, ex-dam workers secured employment at the Smith Lumber Company, and commuted to work from the boomtown area.

The Central Valley area itself attracted lumber mills and retail lumber yards. Two of the largest mills, the Main Lumber Mill and the Rocky Mountain Manufacturing Mill, employed scores of boomtown men. Boomtown developers Wynn Price and Jonathan Tibbitts worked hard to convince the Heron Lumber Mill of Burney to locate a plant in Central

Valley. Price had, by 1950, built and operated a molding mill in Central Valley. Another local resident Art Coggins opened a mill to produce wood shakes employing "mostly ex-dam workers."[9] Subsequently, several more lumber associated mills, plants, and retail lumber yards operated in the boomtown area. Price made a habit of hiring former dam workers and for most of his plant's operation in the 1950s the majority of employees had worked on Shasta Dam.[10] Pete Forte, ex-dam worker, recalled his employment at the Rocky Mountain Manufacturing Plant and at the Main Lumber Company. Forte worked for two years at these plants and remembered that most employees were ex-dam workers and local residents.[11]

Large plywood sheets are visible in this photograph from the post-war era. Mass production of walls and rooftops were now possible in a shorter period of time. With the end of the war, came a huge demand for all types of lumber products in the Bay Area and Los Angeles (Shasta Historical Society).

H. J. (Ike) Geroy remembered being told by fellow dam workers that there would be no more large dam projects to work on and that the lumber business held the best possibilities for future employment. He, as did many former Shasta Dam workers, preferred to stay in the area, enjoying the serenity and beauty of the natural environment of northern California. Geroy like many of his counterparts looked first to obtain a job in local lumber mills or yards. If employment could not be secured in Anderson or at one of the local boomtown mills, ex-dam workers could always try Redding. By 1947 Redding counted ten retail lumber stores, thirteen wholesale lumber yards, two logging companies, four logging equipment and supply houses, and three millworks.[12] By 1950 these Redding plants as well as the Anderson and boomtown area mills helped keep unemployment down to relatively low levels. Local newspapers made note of the "particularly good prospects of obtaining work in the lumber and construction industries."[13]

The lumber boom allowed for readily available and inexpensive finished timber and boomtown residents took advantage of this building opportunity by, in many cases, reconstructing their original, small, and somewhat inadequate homes.[14] This rebuilding period had a profound effect on ex-dam workers. They had been accustomed to small temporary housing, expecting to move on to the next dam job as soon as work was completed on their current project. Now they faced the bright financial future of continuing lumber based employment and the satisfaction of living in larger more permanent homes. Added to this was the fact that many of the workers were raising, by now, one or more children, and they wanted to establish a stable lifestyle. The lumber boom provided the economic base for this stability to occur.

The second largest employer of boomtown residents after World War II was the Bureau of Reclamation. Shasta Dam needed much in the way of finishing work including installation of three huge electric generators, construction of the visitors' center, building the dedication monument and accompanying park, and pouring miles of concrete walkways and driveways. Over 1,200 men were involved in this finishing work on Shasta Dam between the years 1945-1950. In addition to Shasta Dam itself, the Bureau moved to complete the rest of the components of the Central Valley Project—Shasta Division. The immediate concern was for the completion of Keswick Dam to be located nine miles south of Shasta Dam. Keswick Dam would smooth out the uneven water releases from Shasta Dam and power plant. The dam would also generate some electrical current with its own power plant and help contain migratory fish. In addition to Keswick Dam, miles of heavy gauge transmission power lines needed to be strung south from Shasta Dam. The lines required the installation of hundreds of large metal support bases to be erected across the rugged terrain of Shasta County.

LeRoy Hull worked five years at Shasta Dam, from 1945-1950, completing jobs such as interior water pipe installation within the miles of dam tunnels. He recalled that hundreds of workers labored to install the power generators and satisfy the numerous maintenance jobs required.[15] Pete Forte, after returning from active service in 1945 was able to secure a job at the dam helping with the finishing work. He then moved on to

Keswick Dam and continued there until 1947.[16] Forte stated that hundreds of ex-dam workers had been employed by the Bureau and Pacific Gas and Electric to install the power lines extending from Shasta Dam. Many of the men installing the power lines lived in makeshift camps located in remote mountainous areas while their families continued to keep permanent household in Central Valley, Summit City, and Project City. Such was the case with George Van Eaton, who spent five years stringing power lines from Shasta Dam to Tracy, California.[17]

Keswick Dam [pronounced "Kes-ick"] is the after-bay for Shasta Dam. It helps regulate the water flow to the Sacramento River and provides additional hydroelectric power (Bureau of Reclamation).

The Keswick Dam project, in particular, employed significant numbers of boomtown residents. Ray Rogers, a returning veteran, was able to obtain a position as job foreman on Keswick in 1945. He recalled that the overwhelming majority of workers on Keswick Dam were ex-Shasta Dam men. Rogers estimated that several hundred men labored on Keswick, most of those men under his supervision lived in the boomtown area.[18] Dale Bryant was one of the men working on Keswick. He continued to live in Central Valley, commuting to work in a neighborhood carpool. Bryant, like many of those now employed on Bureau water projects, was a returning veteran. Veterans had been promised preference in job selections upon their return, and many men preferred to stay in Shasta County and continue working for the Bureau. Later Bryant and many other ex-dam workers held positions with PG & E for many years.[19]

Other men, like Harold Fortier, finished his job assignment at Shasta Dam and moved on immediately to nearby supporting projects such as the Bridge Bay Bridge and Southern Pacific tunnel work north of the dam site. With rising Shasta Lake, a number of railroad tunnels needed to be relocated and new railroad bridges built. In addition, Southern Pacific continued to hire men for track maintenance.[20]

Maintenance of Shasta Dam itself also employed dozens of workers, many of whom had left for brief stints in the military. Frank Lord, originally a federal dam inspector during the building of Shasta Dam, served a two year tour in the Pacific. He returned to Shasta County early in 1946 and worked as Chief of Maintenance until 1963.[21] Lord recalled most of his men had worked on the dam and had decided to stay in Shasta County. Over half of the maintenance crew had seen service in World War II and used their preferential status to secure a position at the dam.

A large number of the men engaged in Bureau related work continued in that capacity for a number of years as the Trinity River Division of the Central Valley Project moved forward in 1955. Such projects as Trinity Dam and Power plant, Whiskeytown Dam and the Judge Francis Carr Powerhouse, Clear Creek Tunnel and the Spring Creek Debris Dam and Powerplant employed hundreds of workers. These projects extended to 1964 and provided job security for many boomtown families that desired to remain in the area. LeRoy Hull remained employed with the Bureau for many years working on Spring Creek Dam, Clear Creek Powerhouse, and Trinity.[22] Some workers, such as Wilbur Smith, worked for the Bureau on projects outside the area and then returned to Shasta County. Smith moved to Washington after completing his work on Shasta Dam. He worked on the powerhouses at Grand Coulee, but requested to be sent back to Shasta as soon as work became available. Smith moved back to Central Valley in the 1950s where he worked on a variety of Bureau projects, including Trinity Dam.[23]

Job opportunities also existed in Redding. With the construction of Shasta Dam and the subsequent need for commercial support services, Redding businesses expanded. During the period 1938 to 1940 the number of new business doubled. Commercial expansion slowed during the war years, but the lumber boom helped to initiate another business surge that extended through the 1950s. Much of the postwar economic growth in Redding can be attributed to a general optimism that pervaded the nation after World War II. Once initial fears that American industry, both light and heavy, would need many months for a "physical re-conversion" of war related production to civilian consumer production had been dismissed, many hesitant investors and would-be entrepreneurs "took the plunge."[24] One Redding newspaper declaring that area residents were "crying for goods" urged participation by local citizens in Shasta County business ventures.[25] An editorial from the same newspaper warned city planners to recognize the fact that the city's business district would need room to expand. The editorial urged the planning commission to relocate private residents in areas adjacent to the existing business district allowing room for immediate expansion. Commenting that business is "the name of the game" now, the editorial went on to suggest that a competent city manager be hired by the city council to manage the expected economic and residential growth.[26]

Market Street in downtown Redding (1950s) revealed much new business activity. The old City Hall is visible on the left side (palm trees) of then Highway 99. Boomtown residents secured full-time employment in many of the hotels and other service related busnesses (Shasta Historical Society).

As 1946 began, a flurry of new businesses opened in Redding. Most of these new or expanded enterprises sold parts or offered repair services in the mushrooming automobile industry. Now that cars had become available again, many residents invested significant portions of their incomes toward the purchase and upkeep of autos. Herb Gimblin, a Redding resident, opened a large Nash auto dealership. He hired several new salesmen to sell

135

his new and used cars and he employed mechanics (at least one boomtown resident) in his fully equipped garage.[27] The Searways General Repair Shop, Kite's Electric, and the Acme Body and Paint Shop all opened during this time and provided service for area auto owners and job opportunities for several qualified boomtown men. Boomtown men, at least those possessing mechanical skills, found little difficulty in securing jobs in the area.[28] Their training and position as Shasta Dam workers had gained them a variety of experience and the opportunity to master employable skills, and their mechanical and woodworking skills were in demand during the postwar construction and business boom.

The 1950s helped Redding expand rapidly due to improved paved roads that connected rural and remote areas of the northstate. Here we see Market Street complete with drug stores, hotels and restaurants (Shasta Historical Society).

Home construction businesses blossomed and expanded also during this time. Ex-dam workers had considerable experience in pouring concrete and working with electricity and carpentry. These highly trained individuals excelled in securing home construction jobs. B. C Foster Plastering and Concrete employed scores of men to pour foundations and erect brick fireplaces on new homes in the area. Sierra Tractor and Equipment began at this time, and employed many men selling and maintaining construction equipment. Specializing in the big "caterpillar" tractor, then becoming popular for road and housing grading, the Sierra Company employed

136

several boomtown men at the Redding office.[29] Even longtime boomtown resident and promoter Les Pancake expanded his business involvement. Realizing that new home owners needed adequate insurance, he became involved with The Mutual Life Insurance Company of New York and sold both home and life insurance to Redding residents. Pete Forte, a returning veteran who found work in the area, stated that "many boomtown men held jobs related to the mechanical trades."[30] In particular, Forte recalled friends that worked in diesel and truck repair.

Boomtown women also worked in the immediate postwar economy. They had obtained positions in the clerical and light industry fields, and for the most part, continued in these roles. Positions in retail sales skyrocketed following the war as consumer hungry buyers demanded access to household products. As new business starts increased in Redding during the years 1946-1950, employees were needed to stock shelves, help customers, and work the cash registers. Since these jobs paid less than mechanical positions or lumber mill work, most men shunned this kind of labor. Boomtown women realizing that these jobs offered additional financial security for their families, commuted to retail positions in Redding businesses. They scoured newspapers advertisements on a daily basis looking for the best openings. Job opportunities were so numerous that the Record-Searchlight, the newly merged Red- ding newspaper, ran separate help-wanted ads for men and women.[31] Most ads offered jobs in clerical positions or serving as a waitress. Opal Foxx, a boomtown resident from 1942, moved from cooking in the contractor's mess hall to a waitress at various Redding hotel restaurants and eateries, including the Redding Hotel, Jack's Grill, and the locally famous Golden Eagle Hotel.[32] New ethnic restaurants such as Ramona's Place and exciting nightclubs like the newly built Tropics offered employment as well as entertainment.

The opening and growth of large department stores provided another lucrative avenue for job-hunting women. Sears and J. C. Penny both expanded their small Redding stores, hiring mostly women to staff floor and cash register positions. Montgomery Wards completely remodeled their store, adding a full second story. Several boomtown women were hired prior to the grand opening.[33] New clothing stores, including Thompson's Clothes, hired women clerks during the first months of 1946. The department and clothing store boom continued steadily through the late 1940s and boomtown residents remembered neighbors or friends that worked in these stores. One of the largest employers of boomtown women, and Redding women as well, was Pacific Telephone. With a rapidly expanding market in telephone sales and installation, many workers were needed to provide directory assistance and operator information. The Redding office employed dozens of women working on three different shifts. The number of employed workers grew steadily through the 1940s.

Boomtown women sought employment with Pacific Telephone in the hopes of securing good pay and regular salary increases. An advertisement in early 1946 promoted job opportunities at the company stating that "pleasant working conditions, job permanence, and a earn as you learn program" were open to qualified women.[34]

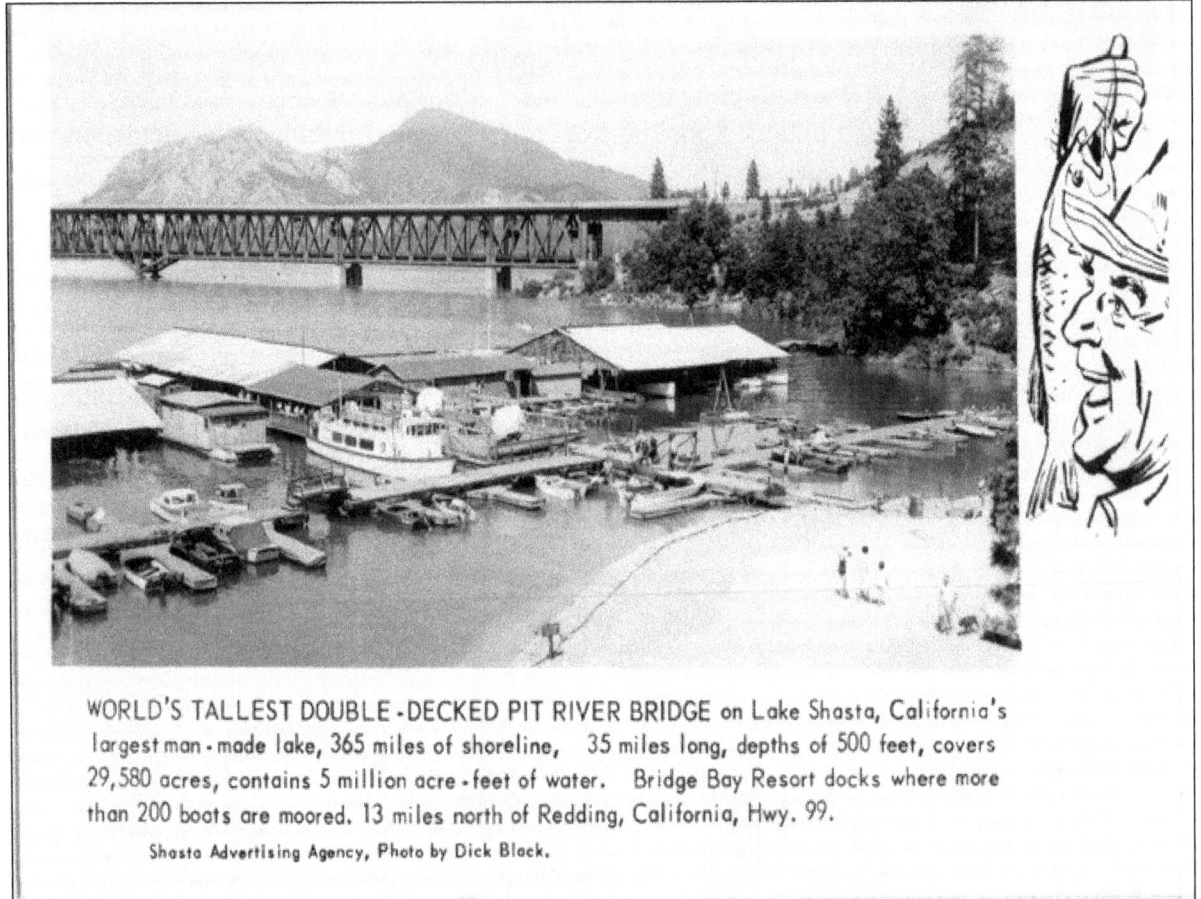

WORLD'S TALLEST DOUBLE-DECKED PIT RIVER BRIDGE on Lake Shasta, California's largest man-made lake, 365 miles of shoreline, 35 miles long, depths of 500 feet, covers 29,580 acres, contains 5 million acre-feet of water. Bridge Bay Resort docks where more than 200 boats are moored. 13 miles north of Redding, California, Hwy. 99.

Shasta Advertising Agency, Photo by Dick Black.

Everyone waited to see the economic impact of Shasta Lake on the boomtowns and Redding. Investment money flowed into development of several lake resorts, one of the largest was [and is] Bridge Bay. Post cards, such as the one shown above noted the natural beauty of the area or the immense human structures—Shasta Dam and the Pit River Bridge (Shasta Historical Society).

While the postwar employment outlook looked bright for boomtown citizens, residents complained about the shortage of water in the area. Ironically, the boomtowns sat only two miles from the then fast rising waters of Shasta Lake, yet a reliable water supply remained an important obstacle to be overcome. Ever since 1938 when over two hundred boomtown settlers pleaded with the Shasta County Board of Supervisors to help supply "water for human consumption" and to sprinkle the dusty streets, area inhabitants experienced water shortages. A large hard-rock

138

strata inhibited attempts at early well drilling throughout most of the area. It was a fortunate homeowner, indeed, who was able to sink a well without great difficulty and expense. Ray Rogers remembered enterprising young men who made a living out of delivering fresh water from the Sacramento River to anxious and grateful boomtown citizens who stored the water in small private wells or barrels. Lack of water forced people to consider relocating as "soon as something else came up."[35] Loral Butcher, a dam worker and local resident, recalled frustration with their situation. Everyone appeared to enjoy their work and the beautiful natural surroundings in which they lived, yet, everyday life became a burden, worrying constantly about the water supply. Butcher agreed with Rogers in stating that residents could not consider the Shasta Dam area as their permanent home until the water problem had been overcome.[36] After spending considerable amounts of money on drilling their wells, boomtown homeowners found mucky water filled with minerals and silt. Filtering to clean the murky liquid proved an expensive and ongoing solution.

A frustrated and tired Pete Moskoff spent a large sum of his earnings in an attempt to sink a successful well. After several attempted drilling episodes, Moskoff finally broke through the rock strata only to watch as a dirty muck oozed out. Large dangerous amounts of iron and other minerals prevented him from using the water. He then spent more money on a filtering system that "took out most of the bad stuff."[37] Another well digging hopeful, Bill Robertson, knew of at least five or six people who had died from breathing poisonous gases released from home water wells.[38] Enterprising Ben Steffens established the first successful water system for the dam area. At first he hauled water from nearby crystal clear streams in the tiny community of Mountain Gate. Steffens' water truck became a welcome sight to thirsty families sweltering in 100 degree plus summer temperatures. Barefoot kids ran behind the truck filling tin cups and jars. Later Steffens filled a hastily built reservoir, and piped usable water to paying customers in Central Valley. The pipes installed in a "haphazard fashion with miscellaneous pipes and materials" broke and malfunctioned often.[39] Steffens' popular reservoir along with his three underground wells supplied only a small portion of the entire boomtown area. Supplies from all sources always ran short especially if the winter rains came late and the reservoir emptied. Searing hot summer conditions dried up much of the local vegetation and any remaining standing water supplies. Early boomtown pioneers, desperate for any type of water, stood in long lines at Steffens pump station. They brought and filled every conceivable container to bring home the precious liquid. Buckets, milk cans, bottles, and construction drums were all used. Matt Rumboltz, Principal at the local Toyon School, recalled hauling water home from Steffens' pump station in a six-gallon garbage can.[40]

From 1940 on Wynn Price and Jonathan Tibbitts, boomtown promoters and residents, attempted to contract for Shasta Lake water. Realizing that a reliable water supply would be critical to further development, Price and Tibbitts formed a committee of concerned citizens and wrote several proposals which they presented to the Bureau of Reclamation. With the advent of World War II, many of the committee members left the area to serve in the military. The federal government, primarily interested in completing the dam, did not take initial proposals seriously. However, at the conclusion of the war and the return of hundreds of veterans, pressure once again was brought on the Bureau to provide water from the now rising Shasta Lake.

In 1948, an agreement was reached and a municipal water system became a reality. The committee formed a legal water district, known as the Shasta Dam Area Utility District. Great jubilation spread across the boomtowns from Summit City to Project City as news of the agreement became public. In a short time, a 15" water line was installed to bring water over the summit from the lake to thirsty boomtowners below. By early 1949 water service had been completed to most homes in the area. Rudi Raki stated that soon after the installation of regular water service, many area residents made the decision to stay in Shasta County, particularly those with children, in secure jobs, or close to retirement.[41] Frances Morrow, married to an ex-dam worker, recalled that solving the water problem led many women to encourage their husbands to remain in the area. Her husband and other men had been talking about the possibility of moving to southern California or to the Bay Area in search of high paying jobs. However, women tired of the dam circuit with its makeshift temporary lifestyle pleaded with their husbands to finally settle down.[42] Morrow noted that with a reliable water source she, and nearly all of her friends, immediately purchased washing machines and other household appliances further adding to the feeling that the communities now offered a lifestyle worth staying for.

As 1950 approached, the Bureau of Reclamation had nearly completed all of the finishing work around the gigantic dam and accompanying powerhouse, and planned a special dedication ceremony. Government officials poured into Redding and thousands of out-of-the-area guests arrived to witness the dramatic opening of the drum gates, the traditional symbolic conclusion to building a dam. Actor Danny Kaye and other Hollywood celebrities performed while Bureau representatives spoke of the many benefits that the dam would provide for all of California. Scattered through the huge throng of onlookers were most of the boomtowners. Many were reminiscing about the "good old days" when life in the boomtowns presented challenges every day. Others cried, sad that they were witnessing the conclusion of the building of the last big dam in

America. Still others felt tremendous pride, a pride in having played a role in this momentous endeavor.

The dam dedication marked, for many boomtown residents the symbolic end to a temporary lifestyle in a temporary community. From now on they would live in the permanent communities of Summit City, Project City, and Central Valley. There was even continual talk about some day incorporating the three communities into one larger city. Pete Forte was there that day and he remembered how the dam dedication fused a community spirit into the hearts of his friends and neighbors. He made a pledge then and there that he would live in the area and retire there.[43] H. J. (Ike) Geroy claimed that the dam dedication moved him in a most dramatic way. He had volunteered to help park cars and direct visitors for the ceremony, and he recalled the intense feeling of pride when asked if he had helped to build the giant dam. Geroy admits today that he and others simply wanted to live near "their dam."[44] Later that night as he drove back from the ceremony to his modest boomtown home Geroy noticed that most of the original tarpaper shacks of the early boomtown days had disappeared and had been replaced by more permanent dwellings. He realized for the first time that Central Valley was truly a permanent community.

Epilogue

In the years following 1950, the Shasta Dam area grew slowly but steadily despite the fluctuating economic environment, Total aggregate population for the three boomtowns had risen to 6,500 by 1980. The 1980 figures break down as follows: Summit City 1,139, Project City 1,659, and Central Valley 3,424.[1] By 1993 the population soared to 9,800 and talk of incorporation grew.

Through the 1950s, a somewhat fluid situation existed and some people moved out as many more moved into the area. Everett Lee found the entire period between 1945 and 1970 to be a time of great movement, with one in five Americans changing residence, and one in fourteen locating in a new county.[2] Good job opportunities remained in the Bay Area and Los Angeles, and word of high paying positions always circulated among those who remained at the dam site.

While some new commercial growth did occur in Central Valley and Project City, Summit City businesses began to decrease in number. Summit City's businesses had focused on supplying entertainment and liquor for the dam workers, particularly single men. By 1960 beer halls, dance halls, and pool halls were no longer in great demand. Most single men who had worked on the dam, were now married or, had moved away. Fortunately, Central Valley had built up a core of family oriented businesses such as restaurants, furniture stores, grocery stores, and supply houses. Project City survived commercially and even thrived due, at least in some part, to its proximity to Highway 99, later Interstate 5. Tourists from both north and south drove first through Project City on their way to Shasta Dam and lake.

With the coming of the 1960s and 1970s, job commuting to Redding became more and more a vital factor in economic opportunities. Redding continued to expand rapidly and assume the role of regional commercial center. The advent of the interstate highway system brought an increased flow of people and goods through the city. Industrial jobs continued also as the huge wood processing plants south of Redding expanded their operation. For a while it appeared that most of the future growth might be south of Redding, leaving the boomtowns with only a claim to supporting recreational tourism for Shasta Lake. Meanwhile, hundreds of dam area residents continued to commute to these industrial jobs and to retail employment opportunities in Redding's growing businesses.

The 1970s witnessed an economic slowdown in Shasta County, part of the general recession caused by the oil embargo of 1974. A slow, yet perceptible change swept over the boomtowns. Toward the end of the decade and into the 1980s more and more ex-dam workers began to retire, living on their social security benefits. Forced to survive on a limited set income, they spent less in nearby stores, and retail sales in the area decreased. Meanwhile, numerous young people began moving into available homes in the area, due to the low cost of housing there. Like their older counterparts, young working men and women commuted to jobs in various locations around Shasta County, particularly in Redding.

The older residents, most of them original boomtown inhabitants now living in retirement, socialized within a well-knit and highly organized network of community events. The highlight celebrations for these older boomtown veterans was, and is today, the annual Central Valley Damboree celebration and parade, and the Shasta Dam Worker's Reunion. These well-planned events reunite many of the local residents with their old friends and fellow ex-dam workers from around the country.

The fate of Toyon was decided (1989). For a number of years the government camp continued to house federal officials overseeing work on Bureau projects in northern California. In the 1960s, after alternately serving as a center for Civilian Conservation Corps activity and being unoccupied, the federal government allowed local Wintu Indians to live in the camp. The Indians renamed the 62-acre site the Toyon-Wintu Center. During the 1980s, the Wintu asked for federal recognition of their tribe and hoped to obtain the Toyon site as a permanent Indian community. However, after several years of occupation that included a stormy relationship with federal authorities, government marshals issued eviction notices. The primary complaint against the Indians was for non-payment of utility bills. In 1986, electricity, water, and sewer services were cut to the community. The Indians continued to reside on the site until 1989 when the government peacefully evicted the remaining dozen or so residents. Tractors and bulldozers moved in and razed the dilapidated homes, outbuildings, and the historic administration building.[3] At present [2011], the Toyon site is in a political limbo, as the Wintu continue court action to obtain tribal status and rights of occupation.

For the boomtowns, on the other hand, the future looked bright as the 1990s opened. Population growth and commercial expansion from nearby Redding spread northward toward the Shasta Dam area. By 1993 several exclusive residential areas, composed mainly of retired couples from southern California and the Bay Area, have been built south and east of Project City. Plans are before the Redding Planning Department to build a huge sprawling shopping mall complex at a location two miles south of the boomtowns.

The 230-acre Shasta Gateway Industrial Park built by the Shasta Dam Area Public Utility District and federal grant money began attracting new businesses to the area by 1993. At least one of the new companies taking up residence in the industrial park relocated from the Bay Area where expansion costs were already much too high. These increasing business transplants could well be the wave of the future for economic growth in the Shasta Dam area.

In September of 1992 residents of the Shasta Dam area voted to form the Gateway Unified School District, taking their high school out of the Shasta Union High School District. This event gave more impetus to groups in favor of incorporation. A citizens group began studying all facets of forming a general law city. The Shasta Dam Area Public Utility board voted to pay for a feasibility study.

On March 5, 1993, a compromise between incorporation supporters and county officials called for the proposed city to repay the county over $400,000 for improvements in the Shasta Dam Area Redevelopment Project consisting of traffic lights at Shasta Dam and Cascade Boulevards and straightening Ashby Road near the Shasta Gateway Industrial Park.

On March 8, 1993, the Shasta County Local Agency Formation Commission (LAFCO) approved the compromise agreement for incorporation. Shasta County Supervisors adopted a resolution calling for an election to be held on June 8, 1993. The new city would incorporate the old communities of Project City, Summit City, Pine Grove, and Central Valley. The voters were given a choice between five names for the new city. They were: Lassen View, Mountain Lakes, Shasta Heights, Shasta Dam, and Shasta Lake. Helen Fisher, a 17-year old resident of Central Valley summed up most residents' feelings on the name issue, "You hate to give up the name you've known
...anything with 'Shasta' in it should do it."[4]

In anticipation of incorporation, the Shasta Dam Area Redevelopment Agency (RDA) planned to move forward with "significant projects that are designed to improve the way we live and create new employment opportunities."[5] Some of the new improvements included realigning and re-grading older intersections and streets, revitalizing Shasta Dam Blvd. with curbs, gutters, and sidewalks, build new parks, rehabilitate older homes, and most importantly develop a new town center on Shasta Dam Blvd.

On June 9, 1993 with about 60% of the registered voters participating the boomtown era finally ended and a new California city was created, Shasta Lake City. Kay Kobe, a business owner and resident of Central Valley, expressed emotions felt by many boomtown residents, "A new city, Wow. We're on to bigger and better things now."[6]

Notes and References

Chapter 1 Central Valley Project

[1] Edward Petersen, *Redding: The First Hundred Years*, (Redding: Norcal Printing, 1972), P. 45.

[2] *The Shasta Courier* (Redding), Sept. 23, 1932, p. 3.

[3] Petersen, p. 46.

[4] *The Shasta Courier* (Redding), April 16, 1933, p. 1.

[5] U. S. Bureau of Reclamation, "Central Valley Project," Fact Sheet—Central Valley Division, Sacramento, CA., 1978.

[6] Donald Worster, *Dust Bowl*, (Cambridge: Oxford, 1979), p. 236.

[7] William Warne, *The Bureau of Reclamation*, (New York: Praeger, 1973), p. 154.

[8] Ibid.

[9] Robert Kelley, *Battling the Inland Sea: American Political Culture, Public Policy, & the Sacramento Valley*, 1850-1986, (Berkley, Univ. of Calif. Press, 1989), p. 308.

[10] Ibid.

[11] Marion Allen, ed. *Shasta Dam and Its Builders*, originally published by the contracting company Pacific Constructors, Inc. in 1945, 1987 edition by Allen, (Shingletown, CA.), p. 13. Richard Lowitt's assertion that the New Deal appeared too late in California to make a difference seems justified when considering the timelines for the Central Valley Project.

[12] J. C. Magurie, "The Birth of Pacific Constructors, Inc.," in *Shasta Dam and Its Builders*, p. 23.

[13] Joint venture organization, on a somewhat smaller scale, evolved in the early years of federal dam building. The usual trend involved one or two large companies forming a nucleus group, bringing in other smaller companies as specialty jobs were required. Bond requirements were then proportionally calculated to company involvement.

[14] Maquire, p. 25. A detailed look at each of the component companies of Pacific Constructors is available on pp. 49-64 in *Shasta Dam and Its Builders*.

[15] Maguire, p. 27.

[16] Maguire illustrates the complexity of bidding from its conception, through filing, in his chapter in *Shasta Dam and Its Builders*.

[17] See footnote #14.

[18] Viola P. May "Ghosts of Yesterday" in *Shasta Dam and Its Builders*. p.18.

[19] Hazel M. Chapman "My Memories of Kennett and the Old Mammoth Copper Mine" *The Covered Wagon*, (Redding, CA.; Shasta Historical Society, 1988), P. 15. Today Kennett lies submerged 450 feet below the surface of Shasta Lake.

Chapter 2 New Arrivals and Early Settlements

[1] John Wesley Powell, Geographical *and Geological Surveys West of the Mississippi*, 43rd. Congress, 1st Session, House Report 612 (Washington, 1874), p.10.

[2] Donald Worster, *Rivers of Empire: Water, Aridity, and the Growth of the American West*, (New York: Pantheon, 1985), p. 139.

[3] Worster, p. 160.

[4] Gerald Nash, *The American West in the Twentieth Century*, (Englewood Cliffs: Prentice Hall, 1973), p. 26.

[5] Nash, p. 95.

[6] Ibid.

[7] The Six Companies partnership consisted of Utah Construction Co., Morrison and Knudson Co., J.F. Shea Co., Pacific Bridge, MacDonald and Kahn, and Bechtel, Kaiser and Warren Brothers. Their bid of $48,890,000 came in at only $24,000 above the Bureau's minimum requirement. Frank Crowe, Superintendent of Construction and veteran builder, put the bid together; later he would, under the application of a different partnership—Pacific Constructors—bid successfully for the construction of Shasta Dam.

[8] This initial squatter settlement pattern at the Las Vegas-Hoover Dam site was duplicated later at the Redding-Shasta Dam location. In the Redding area, transient job seekers setup camp in-and-around the town, along the Sacramento River, and near the proposed site of Shasta Dam. Both of these early squatter settlement cases appear to display many of the same traits, both in stages of the initial setup and in development.

[9] Joseph Stevens, *Hoover Dam: An American Adventure*, (Norman: University of Oklahoma Press, 1988), p. 54.

[10] Stevens, p. 56.

[11] Stevens, p. 123.

Chapter 3 Toyon (Government Camp)

[12] Lyn Parker was the youngest federal inspector at Boulder Dam, and he lived in Boulder City. Parker arrived in Redding as the first on-site inspector for Shasta Dam and was one of the first to move into the new government camp (Toyon). Much of my comparative analysis between Boulder City and Toyon is based on his letters, photographs, and personal recollections.

[13] Personal interview, Lyn Parker, retired federal inspector for the Bureau of Reclamation, March 28, 1990, Redding, California.

[14] Parker.

[15] Shasta County had by this time the largest number of C.C.C. camps in California and young men by the hundreds worked at one time or another on clearing brush from the proposed lakebed, landscaping, road preparation and maintenance, and other dam related jobs.

[16] Parker.

[17] At least part of the early success of the Summit City boomtown commercial center was due in part to its strategic location near Toyon. With regular paychecks in-hand, government workers and their families spent considerable sums of money in Summit City's saloons, markets, restaurants, and diners.

[18] Parker.

[19] Parker.

[20] Parker stated that most Toyon residents did not complain about the lack of services since the boomtowns quickly took up the slack and hurriedly opened businesses. Also, the proximity of Redding allowed for a relatively easy access to a greater range of services.

[21] Roland Forbes, Personal interview, April 10, 1990, Redding, California.

[22] Matt Rumboltz, Personal interview, September 13, 1989, Redding, California.

[23] Almost all the government men I interviewed reported a preference to shop and seek entertainment in Redding over any of the boomtowns.

[24] Some women residents of Toyon did secure part-time and full- time jobs in the nearby commercial boomtowns or in Redding.

[25] James Dahir, *Greendale Comes of Age*, (Milwaukee: Milwaukee Community Development Corporation, 1958), p. 8.

[26] Dahir, p. 9.

[27] Dahir, p. 11.

[28] Arnold R. Alanen & Joseph A. Eden, *Main Street Ready-Made: The New Deal Community of Greendale*, Wisconsin, (Madison: State Historical Society of Wisconsin, 1987), p. 33.

[29] Alanen, p. 44.

[30] Paul K. Conkin, Tomorrow *a New World: The New Deal Community Program*, (Ithaca: Cornell Univ. Press, 1959). Conklin related that the greenbelt suburban cities that attracted so much attention, both from the public and from academia, played only a small role in Tugwell's overall resettlement program. Over 100 rural resettlement towns were established to house thousands of families. These rural experiments, scattered throughout the nation, fared little better than the greenbelt cities. Costs for establishing and maintaining this program doomed it from the start, and the residents with less resources and job skills than those living in the greenbelt cities needed even more economic help from the government. Conkin, pp.188-189, 331.

[31] Conkin, p. 188.

[32] Conkin, p. 198.

Chapter 4 Shasta Dam Village (Contractor's Camp)

[1] The separation of family homes from the rest of the camp appears to have first developed during the construction of Hoover Dam, where workers planned on spending years of residence.

[2] John Crowe, Frank Crowe's nephew, while working as design engineer on Hoover Dam, laid out the preliminary model for Shasta Dam and the accompanying contractor's camp. Crowe planned for the separation of family residences from the single men's dormitories.

[3] V. May, p. 87.

[4] V. May, p. 126.

[5] Opal Foxx, a mess hall employee, recalled her lively days living with four other women employees in a three-bedroom house at Shasta Dam Village. Since proper bedding was difficult to come by, especially at first, they all slept on canvas wood-framed cots. Interview, Redding, CA., September 30, 1989.

[6] Bob Sass, Tape IV A-3, Redding Museum, Redding CA.

[7] James Allen, P. 35.

[8] James Allen, p. 93. Allen related that companies maintaining towns for a number of years made concerted efforts to remove and eliminate private housing. The question then arises-- Was this an attempt to increase paternalistic hegemony over the workers or sincerely try to negate squalor and provide a higher standard of living?

[9] J. Allen, p. 88.

[10] J. Allen, p. 84.

[11] J. Allen, p. 89.

[12] Statements by Bob Sass, J. J. Lynch, and Margaret Schuette, residents at Shasta Dam Village, personal interview, Redding, CA., July, 17, 1990.

[13] Statements made by numerous dam workers, both residents of Shasta Dam Village and the boomtowns, suggest that the mess hall/recreation hall/commissary served as a social gathering and planning center.

[14] V. May, p. 87.

[15] J. Allen, p. 132. Originally taken from Richins, "Social History of Sunnyside.", pp. 3-4.

[16] Statements by Ella Barbera, Bob Sass, and Margaret Schuette, residents of Shasta Dam Village, personal interview, Redding, CA., July 18, 1990.

[17] J. Allen, p. 133.

[18] V. May, p. 122.

[19] Ibid.

[20] Statement by George Van Eaton, Tape II A-7, Redding Museum, Redding, CA.

[21] J. Allen, p. 104.

[22] Matt Rumboltz, "Boomtown" *Covered Wagon*, (Shasta Historical Society; Redding, CA), 1975, pp. 26-27.

[23] *Toyon Monthly* (Toyon School Newspaper), Jan. 1939.

[24] J. Allen, p. 100.

[25] J. Allen, p. 101.

[26] Lynch, interview, July 19, 1990.

[27] Stevens, p. 140.

[28] J. Allen, p. 100.

[29] Ibid. Originally taken from Cooley, *Story of a Complete Modern Coal Mine*, p. 28.

[30] Lynch, interview, July 21, 1990.

[31] V. May, p. 127. Workers interviewed felt an uncommon pride in their important work and an uncommon bond with anyone associated in the construction process. The well-attended annual reunions attest to the ongoing dedication to this very special group friendship.

[32] J. Allen, p 94. A Time magazine article from 1956 points to one extreme case of company involvement in providing recreational activities and involvement in its worker's children. In Colorado, the Climax Molybdenum Co. equipped the isolated company town with ski tows, a youth center, recreation hall with bowling alleys, library, target range and gymnasium, skating rink, and a T. V. booster to bring in distant stations. "Company Town, 1956" *Time*, April 16, 1956.

[33] V. May, p. 127.

[34] Ibid.

[35] Sass, interview, July 17, 1990.

Chapter 5 Stores and Businesses

[1] Truman Hartshorn, *Interpreting the City*, (New York: John Wiley & Sons, 1980), pp. 2 19-220.

[2] With the completion of Shasta Dam and the filling of the reservoir in 1945, the Kennett-Buckeye Road was renamed Lake Boulevard. The original Kennett Road was narrow and chockfull of pot-holes, uninviting to most passenger cars, but a necessary link during the early years of the twentieth century for copper-mining residents living in Kennett. The Bureau in 1938, widened and graded Kennett Road as soon as it was decided to locate the aggregate conveyor belt (the world's longest) parallel to it.

[3] *Shasta Courier-Free Press*, [Redding], Feb. 9, 1939, p. 8, col.5.

[4] Statement by Grant Magnusson, engineer and dam area resident, personal interview, Redding, California, July 28, 1990.

[5] Rumboltz, p. 22.

[6] Statement by Richard B. Eaton, retired Superior Court Judge and area resident, Redding, California, May 16, 1990.

[7] Western gold mining experience recalled a rich history of boomtown entrepreneurs building and losing business enterprises at every conceivable opportunity. See Duane Smith's *Rocky Mountain Mining Camps*, or Richard C. Wade's *The Urban Frontier*, for general accounts of western boomtown business activity; Joseph Steven's *Hoover Dam*, provides examples of boomtown business activity in Boulder City and Las Vegas.

[8] Marion Allen, *Hoover Dam*, p. 7.

[9] *Shasta Courier-Free Press* [Redding], Aug. 20, 1938, P. 2, col. 4.

[10] Rumboltz, p. 22.

[11] Rumboltz, p. 24.

[12] *Shasta Courier-Free Press* [Redding], Sept. 3, 1938.

[13] *Shasta Courier-Free Press* [Redding], July 21, 1938.

[14] *Shasta Courier-Free Press* [Redding], July 28, 1938.

[15] *Searchlight* [Redding], May 29, 1938, p. 4, cols. 3-5.

[16] *Searchlight* [Redding], May 22, 1938, p. 4, col. 1.

[17] *Searchlight* [Redding], May 29, 1938, p. 4, col. 4.

[18] *Shasta Courier-Free Press* [Redding], Dec. 15, 1938, p. 4, col. 4.

[19] *Shasta Courier-Free Press* [Redding], Dec. 15, 1938, p. 4, col. 3.

[20] *Shasta Courier-Free Press* [Redding], Dec. 15, 1938, p.4, col.5.

[21] *Searchlight* [Redding], June 5, 1938, p. 4, col. 5.

[22] *Searchlight* [Redding], April 8, 1938, p. 6, col. 2.

[23] *Record* [Redding], Nov. 8, 1938, p. 6, col. 2.

[24] *Record* [Redding], Nov.18, 1938, p. 3, col. 2.

[25] *Shasta Courier-Free Press* [Redding], Aug. 4, 1938, p. 3, col. 3.

[26] *Shasta Courier-Free Press* [Redding], Aug. 4, 1938, p. 3, col. 1.

[27] *Shasta Courier-Free Press* [Redding], Aug. 20, 1938, p. 3, cols. 4-5.

[28] Low order goods are, according to German geographer Walter Christaller, goods that are frequently replenished, usually displayed in terms of a small locally owned grocery store, eatery, or dry goods shop. More specialized items, such as appliances, automobiles, or furniture would be available in high order threshold centers. Once established, towns offering higher order goods and services tend to attract more high order type businesses, thus monopolizing high order economic development. See Hartshorne, pp. 106-108.

[29] *Shasta Courier-Free Press* (Redding), July 21, 1938, p. 3, col. 6.

[30] Rumboltz, p. 22.

[31] *Shasta Courier-Free Press* (Redding), March 23, 1938, p.4, cols. 4-8.

[32] Information taken from photograph appearing in the Rumboltz article, p. 21.

[33] *Record* (Redding), November 4, 1938, p. 4, col. 4.

[34] The active sponsors belonging to the incorporation committee read like a Who's Who of Central Valley's leading businessmen or early (1937) settlers owning considerable property. They included: Dr. Donald Marchus, Gene Hammans, Walter Poley, D. W. Agnew, F. J. McDonald, W. J. Barton, and Charles Walters.

[35] California state law required a minimum population of 500 in order to be eligible to incorporate. As concern spread in the Redding area, exaggerated population figures appeared, falsely declaring that thousands of "dam workers" were now in residence in Central Valley.

[36] *Record* (Redding), November 12, 1938, p. 1, col. 8.

[37] Ibid.

[38] *Record* (Redding), November 17, 1938, p. 2, col. 4.

[39] *Record* (Redding), January 7, 1939, p. 1, col. 6.

[40] *Record* (Redding), December 19, 1938, p. 1, cols. 4-7.

[41] *Record* (Redding), December 20, 1938, p. 1, col. 6.

[42] Statement by Rudi Raki, boomtown resident, personal interview, Central Valley, CA., September 30, 1989.

[43] Statement by Opal Foxx, boomtown resident, personal interview, Central Valley, CA., September 30, 1989.

[44] Smith, p. 102.

[45] *Record* (Redding), January 11, 1939, p. 3, col. 5.

[46] *Record* (Redding), November 5, 1938, p. 6, col. 7.

[47] *Record* (Redding), January 13, 1939, p. 2, cols. 4-8.

[48] *Record* (Redding), November 17, 1938, p. 6, col. 8.

[49] Statement by Loral Butcher, boomtown resident, personal interview, Central Valley, CA., September 30, 1989.

Chapter 6 Residential Development

[1] Rumboltz, p. 21.

[2] *Shasta Courier-Free Press* (Redding), July 24, 1937, p. 5, col. 8.

[3] Diestelhorst's decision to build in the north Redding area above the Sacramento River encouraged others to do the same, and in effect laid the groundwork for most of Redding's future growth.

[4] Presumably, "unrestricted sections" allowed for areas in which less building code restrictions were applied. Trailers, tar-paper shacks, and even automobiles served as semi-permanent residences for many of these buyers.

[5] *Searchlight* (Redding), March 24, 1938, p. 1, col. 5.

[6] Ibid.

[7] Ibid.

[8] *Searchlight* (Redding), April 24, 1938, p. 4, col. 1.

[9] *Searchlight* (Redding), May 8, 1939, p. 4, cols. 6-7.

[10] *Shasta Courier-Free Press* (Redding), August 8, 1938, p. 4, col. 2.

[11] *Shasta Courier-Free Press* (Redding), September 8, 1938, p. 5, col. 8.

[12] Rumboltz, p. 26.

[13] *Shasta Courier-Free Press* (Redding), December 8, 1938, p. 1, col.2.

[14] *Record* (Redding), November 13, 1938, p. 6, col. 1.

[15] *Record* (Redding), November 12, 1938, p. 1, col. 7.

[16] *Record* (Redding), January 3, 1939, p. 6, col. 5.

[17] Statement by Dale Bryant, personal interview, Redding, CA., September 30, 1989.

[18] Statement by Anderson Pike, personal interview, Redding, CA., September 30, 1989.

[19] Statement by Francis Morrow, personal interview, Redding, CA., September 30, 1989.

Chapter 7 Life in the Boomtowns

[20] Rumboltz, p. 32. Otto S. Hoiberg in *Exploring the Small Community* (1955) stated that high mobility acts as a counterforce in achieving community cohesion, "people who are here today and gone tomorrow, ordinarily do not sink roots." The case with the dam

workers however, reveals frequent mobility, yet a strong community identity would be established in all the Shasta Dam area boomtowns.

[21] Statement by Pete Moskoff, boomtown resident, personal interview, Central Valley, CA., September 30, 1989.

[22] Statement by Loral Butcher, boomtown resident, personal interview, Central Valley, CA., September 30, 1989.

[23] Statement by Charles Barros, boomtown resident, personal interview, Central Valley, CA., September 30, 1989.

[24] Barros, interview.

[25] Statement by Ray Rogers, dam worker and boomtown resident, personal interview, Central Valley, CA., September 30, 1989.

[26] Statement by Dale Bryant, dam worker and boomtown resident, personal interview, Central Valley, CA., September 30, 1989.

[27] Statement by Harold W. Fortier, dam worker and boomtown resident, cassette tape, W-A4, Redding Museum, Redding, CA.

[28] Statement by L. T. Thorton, dam worker and boomtown resident, personal interview, Central Valley, CA., September 30, 1989.

[29] Statement by Matt Rumboltz, Toyon Principal and boomtown resident, personal interview, Redding, CA., June 16, 1989.

[30] *Shasta Courier-Free Press*, (Redding), December 9, 1938, p. 4, col. 5.

[31] Rumboltz, p. 32.

[32] Ibid.

[33] Statement by Jonathan Tibbitts, boomtown resident, personal interview, Redding, CA., June 17, 1989.

[34] Rumboltz, interview.

[35] *Toyon Flashes*, (Toyon School Newspaper), November 9, 1938.

[36] Viola May, p. 129.

[37] *Toyon Monthly*, (Toyon School), February 17, 1939.

[38] Rumboltz, p. 28.

[39] *Toyon Monthly*, December 15, 1938.

[40] *Shasta Courier-Free Press*, (Redding), May 4, 1938, p. 1, col. 2.

[41] *Redding Record*, November 18, 1938, p. 4, col. 4.

[42] *Redding Record*, January 7, 1939, p. 6, col. 6. The PTA voted that night to establish a cordial and cooperative link with PTA groups in Redding.

[43] *Toyon Flashes*, May 28, 1940.

[44] *Toyon Monthly*, March 10, 1939.

[45] *Searchlight*, February 8, 1940, p. 6, col. 2.

[46] Rumboltz, p. 30.

[47] Statement by Frances Morrow, boomtown resident, personal interview, Central Valley, CA., September 30, 1989.

[48] *Searchlight*, August 4, 1938, P. 3, col. 5.

[49] *Shasta Courier-Free Press*, September 12, 1938, p. 1, col. 7.

[50] Rumboltz, p. 30.

[51] Statement by Adah Hubbard, boomtown resident, personal interview, Central Valley, CA., September 30, 1989. At the time of the interview, Adah, at age 93, quickly recalled in sharp detail life in the boomtowns for women. She also remembered the important role that pep clubs played in women's lives.

[52] *Toyon Monthly*, February 10, 1939.

[53] *Searchlight*, March 28, 1940, p. 3, col. 4.

[54] *Shasta Courier-Free Press*, December 15, 1938, p. 4, col. 3.

[55] Statement by Bob Sass, dam worker, personal interview, Central Valley, CA., September 30, 1989.

[56] Ibid.

[57] Rogers, interview.

[58] Fortier, interview.

[59] Butcher, interview.

[60] Sass, interview.

[61] Statement by Pete Forte, boomtown resident, personal interview, Central Valley, CA., September 30, 1989.

[62] Statement by Walter Kuehne, boomtown resident, personal interview, Central Valley, CA., September 30, 1989.

Chapter 8 The Impact of Redding and World War II

[1] Nodal Regions are those hinterlands surrounding a city, typically within a radius of 100 miles; these regions rely on the economic, political, and social support or an already established urban area.

[2] Hartshorne, p. 88.

[3] Taken from Hartshorne, p. 49. reference to Brian L. Berry "Hierarchical Diffusion; The Basis of Developmental Filtering and Spread in a System of Growth Centers" in *Growth Centers and Regional Development*, pp. 108-138.

[4] Statement by Loral Butcher, boomtown resident, personal interview, Central Valley, CA., September 30, 1989.

[5] Statement by George Van Eaton, boomtown resident, Audio Tape II-A7, Redding Museum, Redding, CA.

[6] Statement by Opal Foxx, boomtown resident, personal interview, Central Valley, CA., September 30, 1989.

[7] Statement by Frances Morrow, boomtown resident, personal interview, Central Valley, CA., September 30, 1989.

[8] Statements by Bill Roberston and LeRoy Hull, boomtown residents, personal interview, Central Valley, CA., July 17, 1989.

[9] Butcher, interview.

[10] *Record*, [Redding], December 29, 1938, p. 1, col. 8.

[11] Ibid.

[12] Ibid, December 2, 1938, p. 2, col. 8.

[13] Ibid, December 31, 1938, p.1, cols. 5-6.

[14] Ibid.

[15] Stevens, p. 222.

[16] Wiley & Gottlieb, p. 122.

[17] Statement by Pete Forte, boomtown resident, personal interview, Central Valley, CA., September 30, 1989.

[18] Ibid.

[19] Wiley & Gottlieb, p. 28.

[20] Nash, *American West*, p. 28.

[21] Ibid.

[22] When America entered World War II the dam working population stood between 3,000 and 4,000 workers engaged in all phases of the project. This includes the dam itself, conveyor belt, gravel pits, railroad relocation, power lines, grading, and clearing vegetation from the reservoir site.

[23] Statement by Bob Sass, Audio Tape IV-A3, Redding Museum, Redding, CA.

[24] Ibid.

[25] Statement by Grant Magnusson, boomtown resident, personal interview, Central Valley, CA., July 20, 1990.

[26] Statement by Walter Kuehne, boomtown resident, personal interview, Central Valley, CA., September 30, 1989.

[27] Statement by Leonard Groves, boomtown resident, personal interview, Central Valley, CA., September 30, 1989.

[28] Kuehne, interview.

[29] Statement by Rudi Raki, boomtown resident, personal interview, Central Valley, CA., September 30, 1989.

[30] Groves, interview.

[31] Statement by Pete Moskoff, boomtown resident, personal interview, Central Valley, CA., September 30, 1989. Moskoff and several others remarked that it was considered unpatriotic to waste gasoline.

[32] Dozens of persons interviewed related the effect of gas rationing on their social lifestyle. They affirmed the belief that the war effort demanded a strict compliance to the gas rationing rules.

[33] Bill Roberston, interview. Roberston stated that even friends would "get down on you" for not using the volunteer carpooling system. Anyone driving alone and on a non-work related outing would be accused of driving an "axis taxi."

[34] *Toyon Memories Yearbook*, Toyon School, 1944.

[35] Foxx, interview.

[36] Ibid.

[37] Statement by Estelle Hedstrom, boomtown resident, personal interview, Central Valley, CA., September 30, 1989.

[38] Statement by Vivian Jencks, boomtown resident, personal interview, Redding, CA., July 10, 1990.

[39] Marion Allen, p. 172,

[40] Peterson, pp. 48-49.

[41] William A. Johnson, "Random Thoughts," *Shasta Dam and Its Builders*, p. 159.

[42] Kuehne, interview.

Chapter 9 The Postwar Years, 1945-1950

[1] *The Logger-Tiddings* [Fall River Mills], April 27, 1950, p. 1, col. 2.

[2] Ibid, February 16, 1950, p. 2, col. 4.

[3] Statement by Wilbur Smith, Audio Tape I-A4, Redding Museum, Redding, CA.

[4] Statement by Bob Heikka, Audio Tape TV-A4, Redding Museum, Redding, CA.

[5] Ibid.

[6] Kuehne, interview.

[7] Rogers, interview.

[8] Foxx, interview.

[9] Forte, interview.

[10] Rogers, interview.

[11] Forte, interview.

[12] Al Rocca, "The Shasta Dam Boomtowns," *Covered Wagon*, 1988, p. 24.

[13] *Logger-Tiddings*, March 16, 1950, P. 1, col. 3.

[14] Kuehne, interview.

[15] Hull, interview.

[16] Forte, interview.

[17] Van Eaton, Tape.

[18] Rogers, interview.

[19] Statement by Dale Bryant, boomtown resident, personal interview, Central Valley, CA., September 29, 1990.

[20] Statement by Harold Fortier, Audio Tape IV-A4, Redding Museum, Redding, CA.

[21] Statement by Frank D. Lord, Audio Tape I A-2, Redding, Museum, Redding, CA.

[22] Hull, interview.

[23] Smith, Audio Tape.

[24] *Record-Searchlight* [Redding], January 5, 1946, p. 4, cols. 1-2.

[25] Ibid.

[26] Ibid, p. 5, cols. 1-3.

[27] Ibid, January 4, 1946, p. 8, cols. 6-7.

[28] Out of 119 surveyed dam workers and boomtown residents nearly all found employment in the area. Less than twenty moved away in search of higher wages or particular positions.

[29] *Record-Searchlight*, [Redding], January 4, 1946, p.4, cols. 7-8.

[30] Forte, interview.

[31] *Record-Searchlight*, [Redding], January 8, 1946, p. 7, col. 1.

[32] Fox, Audio Tape.

[33] *Record-Searchlight*, [Redding], January 8, 1946, p. 5, cols. 6-7.

[34] Ibid, January 4, 1946, p. 5, cols. 5-6.

[35] Rogers, interview.

[36] Butcher, interview.

[37] Moskoff, interview.

[38] Roberston, interview.

[39] Rumboltz, p. 26.

[40] Ibid.

[41] Raki, interview.

[42] Morrow, interview.

[43] Forte, interview.

[44] Statement by H. J. (Ike) Gercy, boomtown resident, personal interview, Redding, CA., July 17, 1990.

Epilogue

[1] Population estimates based on figures derived from Rand McNally's *Commercial Atlas and Marketing Guide*, Chicago, 1989.

[2] Everett S. Lee, *Population Estimates: Methods for Small Area Analysis*, (Beverly Hills: Sage Pub., 1982), p. 16.

[3] *Record-Searchlight* [Redding], August 26, 1989, p. 1, cols. 2-8.

[4] Record-Searchlight [Redding], May 30, 1993, p. 1, col. 8.

[5] Shasta Lake News [Central Valley], May 27, 1993, Vol. 1, Issue 2, p. 1.

[6] Record-Searchlight [Redding], June 9, 1993, p.1, col. 5.

Index